Myths and Legends
of
Cornwall

Craig Weatherhill and Paul Devereux

Published by Sigma Leisure – an imprint of
Sigma Press, 1 South Oak Lane, Wilmslow, Cheshire SK9 6AR, England.

British Library Cataloguing in Publication Data
A CIP record for this book is available from the British Library.

ISBN: 1-85058-317-X

Typesetting and Design by: Sigma Press, Wilmslow, Cheshire.

Cover picture: Chun Quoit - midwinter (P. Devereux)

Printed by: Manchester Free Press

Preface

The fame of Cornwall as the home of legends is world-wide. Even as far away as Italy, it was common for the story-teller to preface his tale of the fantastic and supernatural with the words: *"C'era una volta un castello in Cornovaglia"* ("There was once a castle in Cornwall"), and the listeners instantly knew that they were about to be plunged into the world of ancient myth and legend.

It is often the case that such a reputation is in reality undeserved, but Cornwall's sheer wealth and diversity of surviving myths and legends is truly staggering. The main reason for this is simple. Cornwall, or Kernow to give its native name, is still a Celtic land; one of six whose heritage of lore and legend is equally rich.

The bardic traditions of the Celtic lands, in which such tales were committed to memory and retold to a gathered host, lasted in Cornwall well into the 19th century. By this time, the accompaniment of the harp had gone and the bard – or, in Cornwall, the 'droll' – had become the man who told tales by the fireside in return for a meal. The demise of the droll should have signalled the end of Cornwall's myths and legends which would have died with them had it not been for dedicated Victorians intent on recording them for posterity.

The first of these was William Bottrell, a highly educated native of the Land's End peninsula, or West Penwith, who salvaged and committed to paper enough of that far western peninsula's legendary heritage to fill the three volumes he published between 1870 and 1880. The best known of the old drolls he sought out and consulted was the old jack-of-all-trades Billy Foss. Others were traced by a fellow academic of Bottrell's, Robert Hunt. In West Cornwall, he was supplied with stories by Bottrell himself, while in the Lizard peninsula Hunt discovered the old blind droll known to all as "Uncle Anthony James", and published his own collection covering the whole of Cornwall in 1881. Margaret Courtney whose "Cornish Feasts and Folk-lore" was printed in 1890 was a third such intrepid researcher who did so much to save this vital part of Cornwall's heritage and, since then, the Federation of Old Cornwall Societies have salvaged a further wealth of old tales and beliefs.

Cornwall, then, is famous for its legends but some may question the use of the work "Myths" in the title of this book. Study of Cornish legends show that some of the tales and traditions are extremely ancient in origin and that behind the giants, small people, faerie folk, demons and witches are shadows of ancient Celtic gods and goddesses, or heroes from a time before writing.

This was recognised in a recent article in the pan-Celtic journal "Carn" by one of Cornwall's foremost scholars, Richard Gendall. The article, written in Late (Modern) Cornish, recognises parallels between Cornish tales and Irish mythology:

"Brossa radn a ore heb dowt pandrew 'banshee', pokeean 'bean sidhe' rag Gothalack ew. An skeeans ew 'benen an bern cow' moy po le, ha 'sidhe' ew leb ma treegaz an 'siog' ... hedda ew 'pobel an bern cow' pokeean 'an pobel vean'. Mokressa 'bean sidhe' desquethaz tha nebonen thew gwarnyez seere a Ankow.

"Barha nye en Kernow, ma an 'sidhe' trelys tha 'vuggo', ha en vuggo henwez Pendeen Vow ma treegaz edn venen heere quethez an gwidn, toane rosen rooz treeth e gwelavennow. Mokressa hye desquethaz, menze reffo e gwethaz ra merwall whrea!

"Ma keen benen, eze tesquethaz war an garack ew criez An Arlothas Worthenack ha hobma aweeth ew heere ha quethaz en gwidn, toane rosen tooz treeth e gwelavennow; ma e desquethianz gon gwarnya a derroga moar",

("Most, without doubt, know what a 'banshee' is; otherwise the Gaelic 'bean sidhe'. The approximate meaning is 'woman of the hollow hill', and the 'sidhe' is where the 'siog' live ... that is, 'people of the hollow hill' or 'the small people'. Should a 'bean sidhe' appear to someone, it is a sure warning of death.

"With us in Cornwall, the 'sidhe' became a 'fogou' and in the fogou called Pendeen Vau in Penwith there lives a certain tall woman dressed in white, carrying a red rose between her lips. If she should appear, any who chance to see her will surely die.

"A similar woman appears on the rock called The Irish Lady and is also tall, dressed in white and carries a red rose in her lips; her appearance warns of disaster at sea".)

"Cornish Myths and Legends" explores the mystic and often shadowy worlds of this ancient Celtic kingdom, from the great giants to the varied tribes of faery folk; from memories of Arthur, greatest of all Celtic heroes, to the coming of Christianity; from realms beyond the grave to the eternal presence and influence of the sea. The powers of Cornish witchcraft are revealed and also the beliefs and traditions of Cornwall's four-thousand year history of tin mining.

Paul Devereux, author of *Places of Power* and *Sacred Landscapes*, looks at the mysterious lights which have featured in Cornish legend for centuries, and at those mysterious routes and trackways which do not appear to have been laid out for the use of humans alone.

The mythology and legends of ancient Kernow are a vital part of Cornwall's cultural heritage. This book appears at a time when the commercial forces of tourism seeks to alter, trivialise and deface that legendary heritage for its own advantage. In the author's view, that heritage deserves protection equal to that enjoyed by more concrete elements of Cornwall's past, its ancient monuments and historic buildings. It is hoped that this book will help to redress the balance and to enhance the reawakening awareness that the veil between our technological world and the other world remains as tenuously thin as it has always been.

Craig Weatherhill
Penzance 1994

Contents

1

The Giants

ST MICHAEL'S MOUNT (SW 515300) is a major jewel in Cornwall's crown, a majestic cone of rock rising 200 feet from the turquoise horseshoe of Mount's bay, with a village and harbour at its base, and a grand castle-like former priory seemingly growing from the rocks at its very peak. At low water, a cobbled causeway joins the Mount to the mainland at Marazion a quarter of a mile away, and it is almost certainly the place referred to by Diodorus Siculus in the 1st century BC (and probably quoting from the voyage of Pytheas c.300 BC) as the "certain island lying off the coast of Britain which is called Iktis" to which the tin-streamers of Belerion (the Land's End peninsula) carried tin in their wagons at low water for shipment to Gaul and, ultimately, the Mediterranean markets. The network of ancient trackways from the tin streaming areas to the Mount still survive, and the name Iktis may have stemmed from the British "ek-tir" (off-land), in the same way as the island now called "St" Agnes in the Isles of Scilly may have been "ek-enes" (off-island) in the days when much of the submerged area between the islands was dry land.

St Michael's Mount is undoubtedly a place of great power as well as presence and is said to sit on an alignment of earth force known as the St Michael ley. Its Cornish name "Carack Looez en Cooz" (grey rock in the wood) refers back to Neolithic times, when it rose from a low-lying forest inundated by the sea c.2000 BC.

Cornish tradition claims that the Mount is artificial, a fortress constructed by the giant named Cormoran who insisted that it be built of white, quartz-rich granite. The transportation of stone to the site was the task of his long-suffering wife Cormelian and the story is told that on one particular day, and not feeling particularly inclined to travel far, she came across an outcrop of greenstone and brought back a great block of it in her apron. The sight of this dark stone being carried back incensed Cormoran who stormed off to intercept the giantess and kicked her so hard as to make her drop the offending stone which has remained where it fell ever since. Today it is called the Chapel Rock, and stands as a geological anomaly at the Marazion end of the causeway.

St Michael's Mount, home of the giant Cormoran (P. Devereux)

Another legend of the giants of the Mount indicates a link between it and the abrupt, rocky hill of TRENCROM (SW 518362), four miles to the north. Cormoran and Trecrobben, the Trencrom giant (the name is a variant of Trencrom) shared the use of a single cobbling hammer and were in the habit of shouting across to the other whenever its use was needed. The hammer would then be slung from one hill to the other. On one fateful day, the myopic Cormelian heard her husband shout for the hammer and made her way out into the daylight to watch Trecrobben throw the hammer. Unfortunately, the sudden brightness affected her already poor vision and the flying hammer struck her between the eyes, killing her instantly. The grieving giants raised the Chapel Rock and laid the giantess's body beneath it or, according to one heartless version of the story, they merely rolled her body down the hill into the sea.

Trecrobben, after burying his treasures, grieved himself to death.

presumably, this was also the fate of Cormoran, but stories of later origin made him the victim of Jack the Giant Killer who dug a deep pit and lured the old giant into it. The Giant's Well, beside the steep path winding up from the harbour to the castle, is pointed out as the site of this pit. However, it would seem that this story has been transferred to the Mount from the region of Morvah, and that the giant killer was a very different Jack from the farmer's boy of the later tales, as we shall shortly see.

A gateway of the Iron Age hill fort on Trencrom Hill (C. Weatherhill)

There is another tale in which a giant of the Mount waded a few miles along the coast to steal sheep from the estates of Cornwall's famous magician-alchemist, the Lord of Pengersick, although other versions merely refer to the thief as "someone from the Mount". The thief, attempting his getaway with the sheep slung about his neck, was paralysed by the magician's spell which rooted him to the spot. The Terror of his ordeal can be imagined, with the tide relentlessly rising to his chin and the frightened sheep struggling in panic around his neck. In the morning, as the tide fell again, the magician released him from the spell and let the poor thief go, allowing him to keep the sheep, satisfied that the lesson had been learned.

Bottrell doesn't refer to the giant of the Mount as Cormoran, but as "Careg Cowse", a contraction of "Carack looez en cooz". However, the names Cormoran and Cormelian are fascinating; both contain the archaic and obsolete Cornish word "caur" (giant) but the second element of each name is a plant name. Cormoran, then, means "blackberry giant", and Cormelian is the "clover giant". Could it be that each were nature-spirits or even gods of nature?

Traditionally, the Cornish giants carried six fingers on each hand and six toes on each foot and the legends of giants are heavily concentrated in the western half of Cornwall, particularly in the Penwith or Land's End peninsula. With only a couple of exceptions, the Cornish giants are linked with prehistoric sites. On the flattish top of Trencrom Hill, the great natural carns (Cornish word for "tor") are linked by a great wall of huge stones in what Victorian antiquaries liked to call the Cyclopean style. This would appear to be an Iron Age hill fort, dating from a few centuries before Christ, but it may well have even older origins as a tor enclosure of the Neolithic era. A recent survey of St Michael's Mount has revealed traces of prehistoric earthworks on the island.

Hill forts are prominent in the classic giant legend of West Cornwall, "The Giants of Towednack", which contains elements so old that they must have descended from pure mythology. The tale as recorded from the old drolls is extremely long and involved, very bardic in its nature, and the following is necessarily a precis:

Long Tom of Bowgyheere is transporting barrels of ale by ox-drawn wagon from Marazion to St Ives by the old road when he finds that old Denbras the Hurler has built great stone hedges across the road. Denbras (the name means "big man" and was unfortunately ignored by Hunt who decided to call him "Blunderbuss") was the giant who lived in the castle on the hilltop and who owned vast estates in Penwith. Much feared by the ordinary folk, Denbras was rumoured to have had a number of wives and to have killed them all. The fact was that they died naturally and that Denbras' bark was far worse than his bite.

Tom puts aside his inbred fear of the giant, disputes his right to block the road and challenges him to single combat. Tom's improvised shield and sword are a wheel and axle from his cart, while the pot-bellied, fifteen foot Denbras plucks a "twig", a fair-sized sapling. When Tom sees how old and decrepit the giant is, he relents a little and doesn't fight seriously. His care not to harm the old giant goes awry, and Denbras accidentally impales himself on the axle. The dying giant praises Tom's fairness and bequeaths to him his castle and entire estates.

Tom brings his childhood sweetheart to the castle where they live in primitive luxury. To honour the giant, Tom builds a great dolmen over his grave, perhaps the now destroyed Giant's Rock which stood somewhere near Lady Downs, perhaps on Carn Embla. For Tom and his wife Joan life goes on, and they raise a family in peace. Nosy neighbours are kept away for they haven't yet realised that Denbras is dead and that Tom is the new lord of the castle.

He now continues the giant's work of hedging in the land but a travelling tinner known as Jack of the Hammer disputes Tom's right to block the highway, just as Tom had done with Denbras, and the two decide to settle the dispute in time honoured fashion. Each defeats the other in his own speciality: Tom being the victor in wrestling, Jack easily winning in the art of the staff, and they finish up as firm friends.

Jack sets up home with Tom and his family in the castle. The tinner's agile mind and vast array of talents changes their lives. He discovers great riches hidden in the castle itself, then finds whole new tinfields in the district for the miners to exploit. As a result the entire standard of life in Penwith becomes enriched due to his skill.

They now come under the jealous gaze of the sorcerer, the Lord of Pengersick, but Jack's cunning inflicts the only defeat the magician has ever known.

Jack of the Hammer becomes betrothed to Tom's eldest daughter Genevra and builds a fortified home for them on the hilltop near Morvah. First, though he has to rid Morvah of a troublesome giant and he achieves this by working away at the roof of a shallow mine adit and then luring the giant down the hill until the ground gives way beneath him, catapulting the giant into the pit where he is stoned to death.

The marriage of Jack and Genevra takes place on the Celtic feast of Lughnasa, August 1st, and the wedding feast was perpetuated from then until the early part of this century as Morvah Fair, during which people danced around the now removed capstone of an ancient burial cist called the Giant's Stone, and which was said to mark the grave of a giant – perhaps Jack himself, the Morvah giant he slew, or of another giant we have yet to meet, Holiburn of Carn Galva.

Later, Jack is credited with being a local hero and champion, leading his people to victory against raiders from the sea and wreaking havoc among the enemy with his great hammer. Many of the local families were said to have descended from Jack of the Hammer, particularly the Trewhellas, Tregerthens, Trenwiths, Hoskings and Curnows.

Chun Castle – the house that Jack built (C. Weatherhill)

The fortified home built by Jack of the Hammer is the astonishing stone-built hill fort of CHUN CASTLE (SW 405340), built at around 300 BC and occupied for nearly a thousand years. A surprising link with the legend was found inside the castle in 1925 when excavators found an elaborate smelting furnace, tin-slag and an ingot of tin. The topography of the legend also pinpoints Denbras' castle as the hill fort of CASTLE-AN-DINAS (SW 485350), close to which runs an ancient trackway from Marazion to another major ridgeway track now called the Tinners' Track, but formerly known as the Old St Ives Road.

This legend gives the impression that it was set during the Iron Age, with the giants representing the hill fort chieftains and heroes, but the character of Jack of the Hammer is surely that of the Celtic god of light,

Lugh. Like the Lugh of the Irish myths, he arrives as a stranger to a chieftain's stronghold and displays an array of talents which make him a people's champion. He even originates a Lughnasa festival, and there are faint echoes in his confrontation with the Lord of Pengersick of Lugh's defeat of the powerful Balor.

Blight's drawings of the Bosporthennis Beehive Hut

Jack of the Hammer was almost certainly the Morvah "giant" who, at Lughnasa each year, would make his way through throngs of adoring people to Bosporthennis Croft to conduct secret rituals. The strange monument known as the Beehive Hut at BOSPORTHENNIS (SW 438361), an above ground version of West Cornwall's mysterious Iron Age fogous, might have been the ritual site in question.

There are echoes of other Celtic gods in the figure of Jack, especially Taranis the thunder god, as suggested by Jack's fearsome hammer and strange bull's hide coat which "roared like thunder" when struck.

The magnificent headland of TRERYN DINAS (SW 398220) on the southern coast of Penwith is the site of a large Iron Age cliff castle, fortified by a series of banks and ditches which run from cliff to cliff, and around which legends cluster thickly.

It was a magician giant who conjured the castle from beneath the sea and fixed it in place by a lock consisting of a round boulder in a deep hole from which it could not be withdrawn. It was held that if the boulder was ever removed, the great rocking stone called the Logan Rock would topple from its perch on the headland and the whole castle would sink back beneath the sea. The Castle Lock was in an almost inaccessible place but in 1824 the same crewmen of HMS Nimble who displaced the Logan Rock are said to have also broken open the stone enclosing the lock and removed the boulder. The castle has remained in place but it would seem that at least part of the prophecy was fulfilled.

Den an Dynas ("man of the fort") was another titanic lord of Treryn Dinas and a protector of the local people. Deaf and dumb, this giant reacted to seaborne threats by shattering boulders with his fists and hurling the huge fragments at the enemy ships. His wife was An' (Aunt) Venna, "Aunt, being a local term of endearment, and between them An' Venna and "Dan Dynas" were responsible for erecting the huge land-ward defences.

Another giant and giantess who inhabited Treryn Dinas were childless and adopted a son by stealing one of the many children of their sworn enemy, the giant of MAEN CASTLE (SW 348258), on the cliffs just north of Land's End. As the lad grew to manhood, the giantess, who at any rate was tiring of her indolent old husband, began to fall in love with him. The affair blossomed to such an extent that, in the end, the giantess murdered her husband by knocking him over a cliff. He was not immediately killed but horribly injured. In his dying torment he called upon the gods to avenge him. They answered by turning the murderess to stone and even today, the strangely shaped rock called the Lady Logan rocks slowly to and from in the winter storms as though bemoaning her fate. No-one knows what happened to her lover but in the mid 16th century, John Leland visited Treryn Dinas and wrote that "I heard say that one Myendu was lord of it". Could this have been the young giant whose former home at Maen Castle stands close to a headland called Pedn-men-du, "headland of dark stone", or, just possibly, "Myendu's headland"? This Myendu's name could mean "dark stone" or "black muzzle" – the derivation isn't clear but the spelling seems closer to the Late Cornish word "mein, myne" (stones) than to "meen" (muzzle).

The fortified headland of Treryn Dinas, conjured from beneath the sea by a magician giant (C. Weatherhill)

Holiburn of CARN GALVA (SW 429360) – now misspelt Carn Galver by the Ordnance Survey and the National Trust who now own the hill – was another of West Cornwall's giants who protected his human neighbours from his more savage cousins on the Lelant and Towednack hills. Even so, his neighbours feared him and he would have been friendless had not a local youth taken to visiting him. They passed the time playing the favourite giantish games which invariably involved the hurling of great stones. Holiburn used to hold back a little and let his friend win every now and again, until the fateful occasion when the lad won purely on his own merits. The delighted Holiburn congratulated the youth by patting him on the head, forgetting his own vast strength which caved in the boy's skull like an eggshell. Like Cormoran and Trecrobben, Holiburn grieved himself to death.

Carn Galva, seat of the giant Holiburn (C. Weatherhill)

Carn Galva is a magnificent double-peaked hill whose higher summit consists of a serrated peak of jagged granite, a fitting spot for a giant's stronghold except that no such fortification was known to exist there. In 1984, a severe gorse fire laid the hill bare, revealing the remains of tumbled walls linking the great outcrops of stone. The form of this enclosure closely resembled that on Carn Brea above Redruth – another giant's fort – which was dated in the 1970s to the 4th millenium BC, at that time the oldest known fortified village in Britain. The Carn Galva enclosure might be the lost Castle Anowthan of John Norden c.1600 which he described as "a craggie rock on the topp of a hill nere Sener, upon the north sea, somtyme trenched about, and buylte with stone, as appeareth by the ruynes of the walls".

The Bolster Bank, near St Agnes, gave its name to a giant (C. Weatherhill)

It has been suggested that Holiburn might have been the local nobleman Rialobran whose 6th century inscribed memorial stone stands within sight of Carn Galva.

The giant of CARN BREA (SW 685407) is undoubtedly dead. His sightless petrified head protrudes from an outcrop at the eastern end of this impressive hill, while his hand, also turned to stone, can be found at the opposite end of the great system of prehistoric earthworks which surround two of its three summits. Late tradition gives this giant the unlikely name of John of Gaunt.

It is unclear whether the Carn Brea giant was the sworn enemy of

Bolster, the giant of ST AGNES BEACON (SW 710505) or if the devil was the foe in question. Whichever it was, he so incensed Bolster that the St Agnes giant cleared his hill of stone which he hurled at his enemy in such torrents that Carn Brea is covered with boulders.

Bolster is a good example of a giant being named after an earthwork, in this case the Bolster Bank which runs from Chapel Porth to Trevaunance Cove, thus enclosing a large area of tin-rich land including the entire hill of St Agnes Beacon. The bank is now interrupted in a number of places and an isolated fragment immediately south of Bolster Farm looks just like an upturned boat. The name Bolster is a contraction of "both lester" (boat-shaped hump).

Bolster is claimed by some accounts to have been of immense size, being able to cover the six mile distance between Carn Brea and St Agnes Beacon in one massive stride.

Like so many of his kind, Bolster came to a sad end. He became infatuated with the lovely St Agnes herself and so pestered her that she agreed to return his love if he would prove his own by filling a hole in the rocks with his blood. Bolster agreed and the devious saint opened a vein in his arm to let the blood flow into the hole which, to this day, has red-stained sides. Unbeknown to Bolster, and only too well known to St Agnes, the bottom of the hole opened onto the sea and the gullible giant bled to death.

The hole still exists at Chapel Porth, close to a little grass grown enclosure which once held the remains of St Agnes' chapel and holy well. It is pointed out as "Wrath's Hole", but this is the name of another giant who lived down the coast near Portreath. Here the tall, vertical cliffs are cleft by a fearful sunless chasm called RALPH'S CUPBOARD (SW 645451), once a great cavern occupied by the giant Ralph or Wrath. His pastime was to ambush passing ships, plucking sailors from their decks to satisfy his voracious appetite. If Wrath's name is Cornish, then it is a puzzling one: "(g)wrah" (witch, hag, crone) would be the only word from which it could be derived.

Although there are earthworks on nearby Tregea Hill, Wrath seems to be one of the very few Cornish giants not directly connected with ancient fortifications. Another is the Land's End giant who lived at TREVEGEAN (SW 368294). In 1602, Richard Carew wrote that: "not far from the Land's End there is a little village called Trebegean, in English the town of the Giant's Grave, near whereunto and within living memory (as I have been informed) certain workmen searching for tin discovered a long square vault which contained the bones of an excessive big carcase and verified the etymology of the name". Robert Hunt expanded on this and, not understanding that the G of the place name is soft, decided to call the giant Trebiggan. According to Hunt, the giant was so big that he could pluck sailors off passing ships and place them on the Longships reef. Like Wrath, he enjoyed human flesh, dining on young people fried on a large flat rock near his cave. In fact, the place name Trevegean could indeed mean "farm by the giant's grave" (trea + beath + gean: this last word, pronounced "jee'an", superseded the old "caur" as the Cornish word for a giant).

There are other instances of giant skeletons being found in Cornwall. At TREGONY (SW 925449) the bones of a man 11 feet tall were said to have been found a few centuries ago, and 19th century restorations on St Michael's Mount discovered a skeleton more than seven feet tall in a vault under the castle church. The circumstances here are a little suspect: Dr William Borlase entered this same vault a century earlier and saw nothing of note.

On Cornwall's south coast is the great headland known as THE DODMAN (SX 002395), notorious to all sailors. A huge earthwork called the Hack and Cast runs across the promontory and the fate of the giant who dwelt here closely parallels that of Bolster. This unnamed giant was the terror of the neighbourhood but fell ill one day and roared for a doctor. Seizing his opportunity, the doctor persuaded the agonised giant that he must be bled. Like Bolster, he was duped into letting his blood flow into a hole which opened to the sea. When the giant was sufficiently weakened, the doctor sealed his success by kicking him over the cliff to his death. Some say that the name of the headland means the "dead man"; place-name scholar Oliver Padel suggests the surname of a family who once lived hereabouts, Dudemann. A further possibility is that it might be the Late Cornish "tubmen" (earth bank, dyke), referring to the ancient earthwork.

A creation myth still exists in the north-eastern corner of Cornwall, and concerns the giant brothers Tavy and Tawrage who were both in love with Tamara, a beautiful nymph, daughter of the spirits of the earth, who loved in a cave near MORWENSTOW (SX 206154). Her parents, fearful of the moorland giants, found her in the company of both and cast a sleeping spell upon them, before instructing Tamara to return to the dark caves beneath the earth. Weeping, she refused, and her incensed father cursed her, changing her for all time into a river of tears. When Tavy awoke, he realised what had happened and called upon his father to change him into a river, which flowed alongside and eventually merged with Tamara's stream. Tawrage also sought such magical help but tragically he chose the wrong route so that his river forever flows away from his brother and his beloved Tamara. So originated the Tamar, the Tavy and the Taw.

It is no longer remembered if it was a giant or the devil who was responsible for raising THE GIANT'S HEDGE (SX 141572 to SX 247536), the great linear earthwork which runs between the estuary of the Fowey at Lerryn to that of the Looe River, enclosing a huge tract of country. The old rhyme has it that: "One day the devil, having nothing to do; Built a great hedge from Lerryn to Looe".

At Varfell, between Penzance and Marazion, is the last vestige of another linear earthwork which might have cut off the entire Penwith peninsula, following the line of the present A30. This is the GIANT'S GRAVE (SW 507322), but tradition doesn't recall the giant concerned. However, on studying the topography of "The Giants of Towednack" story, it might have been the work of Denbras the Hurler.

The Cornish giants are particularly noted for their raising of huge earthworks and fortifications, and also for their habit of hurling great boulders about the countryside. The giants have gone but their works remain for all to see. Trencrom Hill still retains the Giant's Well, Cradle and Spoon while in a stream at the northern base of the hill the massive BOWL ROCK (SW 522368) testifies to Trecrobben's games. The natural outcrop called CREEG TOL, overlooking the wonderful stone circle of Boscawen-un (SW 412274) is still deeply indented with the Giant's Footprints and Carn Brea is still richly endowed with its giant's belongings, including his Crocks and Kettles, a massive perched boulder covered with mysterious rock basins.

Also noticeable about the Cornish giants is their apparent lack of intellect which can perhaps be understood if their legends are folk memories of ancient chieftains; after all, our modern political leaders and statesmen are invariably railed for their stupidity by commentators, so this legendary trend could be seen as a kick against figures of authority. However, if our giants are indeed ancient gods, then one can draw parallels with some of the unintelligent acts of, for example, the gods of ancient Greece. What cannot be denied is the indelible mark they have left upon the Cornish landscape.

The Giant's Footprint on the outcrop of Creeg Tol (C. Weatherhill)

2

The Races of Faerie

Cultures throughout the world retain traditions of hidden races of paranormal people, usually small and with characteristics which raise wonder in the minds of mortal folk: the Irish Sidhe; the lios-alfar, duegar and trolls of Scandinavia; Scotland's Seelie and Unseelie Courts and the Tylwyth Teg of Wales to name just a few. Even the North American Indian cultures have them.

For such a small place, Cornwall has an astonishing variety of fair-folk, few of which are shared with English culture. Some are not so fair. Victorian commentators tended to muddle them somewhat, so that one variety becomes featured in a story which is contrary to its general characteristics and should rightly feature another.

PISKEY is a name which springs most immediately to mind whenever Cornish faery folk are mentioned, but there are two distinct varieties. The tourist browsing in Cornish gift shops is assailed with "piskies", usually of the lucky variety. These sprites are most widely found in East Cornwall and seem to closely resemble the Devonian Pixy. Often found in groups, the East Cornwall piskies are mischievous creatures, leading the unwary traveller astray, riding young colts to the point of exhaustion, their manes often being found plaited into tiny stirrups after such a night, or chasing cows.

Their equestrian habits are recorded in the region of LISKEARD (SX 250645) and near the FOWEY ESTUARY. Thomas Couch, in the 19th century, recorded a number of Piskey traditions in the immediate area of POLPERRO (SX 210510), such as the assertion of an old fisherman, Robin Hicks, that the local piskeys took to tormenting him on stormy winter nights by clapping their hands and crying out: "Robin! Robin! Your boat is adrift!". This would be repeated all the way to the quay where the soaked and storm-battered Mr Hicks would invariably find his boat lying safely at its moorings.

John Taprail, a fisherman in the same area, was similarly lured down to his boat on a frosty night, only to find that nothing was wrong.

However, in the shelter of a larger boat on the beach, Taprail spotted a group of the sprites sitting in a semicircle and sharing out a heap of money by tossing coins into the hats laid out before them. Forgetting that such creatures resent being spied on, Taprail craftily pushed his own hat in with the others, then, after the share-out, tried to sneak away with his prize. The piskies pursued him and he only escaped after their clutching hands had ripped away his coat-tails.

Couch also recorded the story of a piskey helping a local farmer by hand-threshing his corn by night. The farmer stole up to the barn to watch him at work and noted that the little fellow's clothing was ragged and old. In gratitude the farmer left a new set of clothes for him the following night but the sprite's reaction was unexpected. After putting the new clothes on, he sang out: "Piskey fine and piskey gay; Piskey now will fly away" (or, in another version: "Piskey new coat and piskey new hood; Piskey now will do no more good"). He never returned, presumably annoyed at having been spied on.

According to Couch, only two of East Cornwall's piskeys are known by name, these being familiar to anyone who has entered a local gift-shop: Jack o'the Lantern and Joan the Wad.

The Dartmoor Pixy is generally described as resembling a pile of old rags but we lack a detailed description of the East Cornish Piskey. Always mentioned as being small, he generally wears ragged clothing of green. As noted above, there are vague mentions of hats, hoods and coats, but beyond this there are few clues as to what they look like and we have to view the gift-shop version with its prominent pointed ears, narrow face, slanted eyes and Noddy hat with suspicion.

Small brown moths are sometimes referred to as "piskey-moths" in Cornwall and it is common advice that blackberries should be picked before Piskey has a chance to "spoil" them (how he does this is best left to the imagination).

Some of the characteristics of the East Cornish piskeys are shared by PISKEY of the Land's End peninsula but he is nevertheless a very different creature. To begin with, there is only one Piskey, a wild, elemental and generally solitary being, although he does interact with the smaller Pobel Vean or Small People.

Apart from a small area at ZENNOR (SW 455385) where he is said to haunt some fields near the church, Piskey is usually to be found in the region of CARN KENIDJACK (SW 388330), legend's notorious "hooting carn", and THE GUMP or WOON GUMPUS, that weirdly flat tract of moorland between Carn Kenidjack and Chun Castle. It was here than An' Pee (Aunt Penelope) Tregeer encountered him in Bottrell's detailed account of her bedevilled trip home to Pendeen from Penzance Market.

First, and like his eastern cousins, he leads the old woman off the road until she is lost then, when she finally regains her bearings, she spies him in an old barn at Boslow, a farm close to Carn Kenidjack, threshing corn for the elderly farmer with members of the Small People helping him. At this point, Bottrell supplies a graphic description of him: "...a little old man, not more than three feet high, covered with only a few rags and his long hair that hung over his shoulders like a bunch of rushes. His face was broader than it was long; she couldn't make out the colour of his great round owl's eyes, they were so shaded by his shaggy eyebrows from between which his nose, like a snout, poked out. His mouth reached from ear to ear, and they were set far back to make room for it. His teeth were very long and jagged and he was so eager about his work that, with each stroke of the threshal, he kept moving his thin lips round and up and down, and his tongue in and out. He had nothing of a chin or neck to speak of, but shoulders broad enough for a man twice his height. His naked arms and legs were out of all proportion, and too long, for his squat body; and his splayed feet were more like a quilkan's (frog's) than a man's".

Having been told in no uncertain terms that, for spying on Piskey he'd "serve her out", the old woman escaped back onto the Gump where exquisite music and a myriad tiny lights led her to a Small People's feast. Disastrously, she tried and failed to steal some of their treasures. Tormented by dozens of pinches and pokes, she writhed on the ground and looked up to see Piskey in the role of arch-tormentor, "mounted on a year-old colt, his toes stuck in the mane, holding a rush in his hand to guide it. There he sat, putting on (egging on) the smaller sprites to torment her, making a tee-hee-hee and haw-haw-haw, with his mouth open from ear to ear".

The demented laughter of Piskey is well-known, giving rise to the Cornish phrase "laughing like Piskey". A sure cure for the piskey-led is to turn an article of clothing inside out but An' Pee Tregeer extracted herself from her ordeal by a more drastic method known as the Adder Charm: the first two verses of the 68th Psalm.

In this account, Piskey gives the impression of being an ancient entity; a nature spirit of the rawest type. It also shows him in his two most familiar guises, that of benefactor to the old and needy, and as mischief-maker-in-chief to the faery tribes.

THE SMALL PEOPLE or POBEL VEAN are a major faery tribe in Cornwall, and thought by some to be the spirits of prehistoric people. Being of pre-Christian origin, and therefore pagan, they were held not to be good enough to enter heaven, but also too good to be condemned to hell. So, they exist in a kind of limbo, slowly diminishing in size so that eventually they become "muryans" (ants) and, in the end, be totally lost. Some even say that they were once Druids.

Treryn Dinas, where the Small People tend their aromatic gardens on inaccessible ledges
(C. Weatherhill)

Generally depicted as being of great beauty, the Small People love to enjoy their own revels, but tend to become demure when aware that human eyes are watching. They often interact with humans, helping the needy and even befriending those people, but are also known to exhibit behaviour towards humankind which is not so sociable by our standards. They are passionately fond of goats, horses and milk cows, and places frequented by goats are often favoured sites for Small People activity.

Although the Small People are creatures of the open coast and countryside, they also favour the old Iron Age hill forts and cliff castles. On inaccessible ledges of the great fortified headland of TRERYN DINAS (SW 398220) they tend their aromatic gardens and play exquisite music which excites the senses of local crabbers at their work. In the western hill fort of CASTLE-AN-DINAS (SW 485350) they hold their fairs, and they are also known to inhabit the fort of CAER BRANE (SW 298291), within whose ramparts nothing evil can walk.

Nothing that is evil can walk within the ramparts of Caer Brane (C. Weatherhill)

Sources generally agree on the size of the Small People, with accounts of them being "half a yard" high, or "not over two feet" tall, the women being less tall then the men. Victorian descriptions tended to clothe them in the garb of gentry, huntsmen or soldiers from a century earlier, with men wearing three-cornered hats, blue square-skirted coats with lace, breeches, stockings and either buckled shoes or riding boots of black or russet. The women are often depicted in long, waisted gowns over hooped dresses of summer flower hues, and high heeled velvet or satin shoes with pointed toes. Masses of jewellery are worn in the form of buckles, brooches, bracelets, rings and beaded necklaces of coloured crystals. If the 18th century style is put to one side, the general details of bright colours and lots of jewellery are reminiscent of the clothing worn by Celtic nobility in the Iron Age.

Their faces are beautiful, the men normally having darker complexions than the women, who have long flaxen curls worn loose or occasionally worn up and styled to an exaggerated height. Their eyes are dark and sparkling and their skins without blemish. It is said that they avoid being seen by day, for then they look aged.

When An' Pee Tregeer saw their revels on that haunted western moor called THE GUMP (SW 397335), they were evidently celebrating the feast of Samhain, for it was Hallan Eve – Hallan being the nearest Sunday to Halloween. Interestingly, some of the Small People were dancing around a nine-foot maypole which was wreathed in flowers. Others were wrestling, gambling or hurling with a luminous ball. It was only when she tried to steal some of their precious plate that they turned on her, with Piskey also in attendance to egg them on.

Different descriptions of the Small People by 19th century eye witnesses in places twenty miles apart agree remarkably. In 1810, a tailor named William Dunn was returning home to Sparnock one night when he came across a procession of Small People near the churchyard at KEA (SW 810427), while in about 1850 dressmaker's assistant Rebecca Noall and her father saw a similar procession at ST IVES (SW 518405). On both occasions, the Small People, again about two feet tall, were beautifully dressed in scarlet cloaks and tall, black, steeple-crowned caps.

In the most famous example of their frequent interaction with humans, that of Anne Jefferies, the Small People were merely "clad in greene". This relationship was described in a letter dated 1696 from Moses Pitt to the Bishop of Gloucester. When young, Anne had been in service to Pitt near her home at ST TEATH (SX 064806) and had first encountered this "small sort of airy people" in Pitt's arbour. At one point she "forsook eating our victuals and was fed by these fairies from that harvest time to the next Christmas day".

The Small People gave Anne the power to heal and this gave John Tregeagle, justice of the peace and steward to the Earl of Radnor, the opportunity to imprison her without food in Bodmin Jail (Tregeagle has his own place in Cornish legend, as we shall see in Chapter 9). Again, the Small People contrived to feed her.

Moses Pitt's account gives a curious instance of the fairies quoting from the scriptures. Anne had been called from the room to her own chamber by voices only she could hear, later returning with a Bible in which a page had been turned down at St John, Chapter 4. The Small People had asked her if priests had tried to dissuade her from seeing what they would call evil spirits and delusions of the devil. They told her to advise the priests to read from verse 4 of the chapter: "Dearly beloved, believe not every spirit, but try the spirits, whether they are of God". What Pitt found remarkable was the fact that Anne could not read.

This tends to contradict the usually held belief that the Small People are mortally afraid of anything to do with Christianity, and so does the story of a Small People tribe burying their queen before the altar in LELANT CHURCH (SW 548378).

A further belief, in common with other Celtic countries, is that the secret of hidden treasure will be revealed if one succeeds in capturing one of the Small People. At TREVESSA (SW 482397), near St Ives, a farmer found one asleep on Trendrine Hill and carried it home before it could wake. The family called the little man Bobby Griglans ("heather"), but a moment of negligence by the farmer's children saw the faery, whose real name was Skillywidden ("white wings"), rescued by his own parents before the secret could be revealed. On the far side of Trendrine Hill, the farm of Skillywadden ("poor nooks") was once claimed to be "named after a faery".

An almost identical story is told of a farm near POLPERRO (SX 210510), but here the faery goes by the distinctly Anglo-Saxon name of Coleman Grey.

The Small People are said to live underground, but some stories suggest that they also exist in a parallel dimension. The best known is that of the lost child of Trefronick, a farm near ST ALLEN (SW 822506) who is led through a tangled wood by a beautiful lady into a place where palaces have glass pillars and arches hung with crystals. He spends only an evening there and yet, when he is found asleep by frantic searchers, several days have passed.

Selena Moor is a shallow, marshy valley, thick with goat willow, to the south of ST BURYAN (SW 410258). Here, Mr Noy was led astray and into a wood he could not recognise. There he found a house and revelling Small People served by a local girl, a former sweetheart who had supposedly died four years previously. The girl, Grace Hutchens, told Noy that she had been changed into faery form and the body buried in St Buryan churchyard had been a changeling corpse.

Fascinating details emerged of Small People society. They were not Christians, but star-worshippers. They did not practice marriage, being too long-lived for a permanent relationship to be practical. In the increasingly rare event of a child being born within the tribe, then any man would be proud to be thought the father (a detail which surprisingly escaped Victorian censorship). In winter they lived in underground realms, entered from carns (tors) and cliffs. Some could shape-shift into animal form, especially into goats so that they could lure other goats into their realm. It was these shape-shifters who suffered from diminishing size, growing smaller with each change until they become "muryans" (ants) and are finally lost, rather than the general belief that all the Small People were shrinking away.

Hints of their subterranean dwellings come from MOUSEHOLE (SW 470265), where naughty children were threatened with being carried into "Dicky Danjy's Holt", a cave to the north of the harbour, by the Small People; and from the story of the greedy old man on the Gump who saw the "hill before him open" and the Small People troop out. As the hillslopes enclosing the Gump are very gentle, it is hard to see where this could have happened, unless the hill in question was a Bronze Age barrow, in other words, a "sidhe".

The Small People hate dirtiness and Betty Stogs of TOWEDNACK (SW 488381) learned to mend her slovenly ways when they stole her filth-encrusted child and left it scrubbed scrupulously clean for her to find.

It might be possible that the Small People occasionally give birth to deformed children, in which case they may swap it for a human child – a changeling. There are various tales of this but the practice is also carried out by the next class of Cornwall's faery folk, the Spriggans.

THE SPRIGGANS are a goblin race purely confined to the weird and ancient landscape of the Land's End peninsula, and the rest of Cornwall can be truly thankful for this. Hordes of these hideous beings infest the megalithic monuments and old hill forts, hissing, spitting and leering horribly. Their name, which is pronounced "sprid-jans", comes from the plural form of the Cornish work "speriz" (spirit), and they are said by some to be the ghosts of the old giants, guarding the treasures hidden by the giants.

The treasure of the giants of Trencrom Castle are guarded by hordes of hideous spriggans
(C. Weatherhill)

A man once searched the old fort on TRENCROM HILL (SW 518362) for the giants' treasure and, on finding a secret mark, began to dig. Immediately, the sky darkened, a gale sprang up and thunder began to roll around the hill. The man looked up and saw, to his everlasting horror, that hordes of spriggans were swarming out of the rocks and rapidly growing from tiny size to huge. The treasure seeker took to his heels, escaped by the skin of his teeth and was confined to his bed for weeks.

These same Trencrom spriggans were notorious thieves and, at one time, chose the cottage of an old woman at CHY AN GWEAL (SW 522390) as a place to divide their spoils. One night, the old woman summoned up the courage to grab the rich booty but, as the startled spriggans ran off, one of them passed his hand over her shift which, from that day on, gave her unspeakable agony whenever she attempted to put it on. Nevertheless, the old lady prospered and spent the rest of her life in comfort.

Whenever unexpected storms spring up, or thick, swirling mists, to blight the crop or spoil the harvest, it is the spriggans who are the cause. If they are the ghosts of the giants, then it is surprising that they can breed for they, like the Small People, often swap their own ugly brats for human children. However, in the best known account of this, the Changeling of Brea Vean, it turns out that the spriggan "child" is, in fact, an adult.

Jenny Trayer (or Janey Tregeer) is working in the fields at BREA VEAN, a farm near the foot of CHAPEL CARN BREA (SW386282), having left her baby at home. When she returns in the evening, her own dear child is gone and in its place is an ugly, wizened brat. The wise-women declare it to be a changeling, almost certainly belonging to "the spriggans who swarm around Bartinney still", and that she should bathe the brat in the holy well of Chapel Euny on the first three Wednesdays of May if she is to hope to see her own child again.

The spell seemed to have no effect. On the first two occasions, the creature roared with malicious glee instead of fear. On the third Wednesday, she was carrying the thing on her back along the old track which led to the holy well when a voice rose from the empty hillside of Bartinney: "Tredril! Tredril! Thy wife and children greet thee well!"

The young woman's terror can be imagined as the creature on her back roared in reply: "What care I for wife and child when I can ride the Dowdy's back and have good pap my fill?"

The wise-women now declared that only drastic action could now work. She must now fling the brat on the ashes pile and beat it black and blue with the heel of her shoe (before she could go too far with this, the shoe was flung from her hand by an unseen force). She must then lay the creature beneath a stile on the old church path and wait for morning. She did so, and there lay her own sweet child.

The child grew to be a solitary soul, delighting in the natural world around him and often conversing with the faery world that only he could see. He became a shepherd, tending flocks on the slopes of

Bartinney Hill. When he was thirty, his flocks were seen wandering and people went to look. They found him on a bed of rushes, apparently asleep, but the Changeling of Brea Vean was dead.

THE KNOCKERS inhabited the tin and copper mines of Cornwall, not unlike the Kobolds of Germany. Some of the alternative names given for these sprites by Victorian recorders like Robert Hunt, "bockles" and "nuggies" turn out not to have been known by Cornish miners at all. William Bottrell provides a graphic description of the faery miners who worked in BALLOWALL MINE (SW 358313), that "queer old bal, that was worked before the Flood" near St Just:

"They were miserable little, old, withered, dried up creatures; the tallest of them no more than three foot six or thereaway, with shanks like drumsticks, and their arms as long, or longer, than their legs. They had big, ugly heads, with grey or red locks, squinting eyes, hook noses and mouths from ear to ear. The one older and uglier than the rest seemed to take the lead in making wry faces and all sorts of mocking tricks. When he put his thumb to his nose and squinted at Tom, all those behind him did the same. Then all turned their backs, stooped down, lolled out their tongues and grinned at him from between their spindle shanks".

These were Knockers who had been annoyed by a miner called Tom Trevorrow who had insulted them and then refused to leave a share of his meal with them, as was the custom. Older miners told him that the levels he'd been working were more infested with "knackers" than any other part of the mine. "Many a night", they said, "these troublesome spirits have been seen whisking round the blacksmith's shop and going down the Buck Shaft that enters the level you are working in. This shaft is so called because a black buck-goat, or a Bucca in the shape of one, was seen to go down there but never found below". When the anger of the Knockers nearly killed him, Trevorrow was forced to leave the mine and find work elsewhere.

Generally, though, the Knockers were benevolent and guided human miners towards productive lodes by the sounds of their working in what seemed to be unbroken rock. Some believed that they were the ghosts of Jews popularly supposed to have been introduced into Cornish mines in the reign of King John or even earlier, or even those who had crucified Christ. It was said that they were forced to sing carols at Christmas time as part of their penance, and are never heard working on the Jewish Sabbath or other festivals. This belief is not ancient and bears all the hallmarks of the anti-Semitic attitudes of Christianity and particularly Wesleyan Methodism in the 18th and 19th centuries.

At the Ransom and Rosewall Mines, on the slopes of ROSEWALL HILL (SW 497393), the Knockers working a particularly rich section formed a partnership with an old miner named Trenwith. Their expertise would mine the ore and Trenwith would bring it to "grass" and see it properly dressed with the agreement that he would leave a tenth of the dressed ore for the Knockers. He kept to the agreement, the lode continued to be rich, and he prospered. After his death, though, the partnership was carried on by his son who sought to cheat the Knockers. The lode failed, he took to drink, squandered all the money his father had made and died a beggar.

Near TOWEDNACK (SW 488381), anyone listening at the mouth of the Fairy Well could hear the Knockers at work far below. A notoriously idle man named Barker took to listening at the well and discovered from the conversations he could hear that the Knockers worked eight hour shifts and, on leaving, they would hide their tools. One evening he heard a voice say that his tools would be hidden in a cleft in the rock; another said he would place his under the ferns, and a third announced that he'd leave his tools on Barker's knee. At that moment a crushing weight fell on the eavesdropper's leg and from that day on, he limped on a stiff knee.

In the Tom Trevorrow story, it is interesting to learn that the Knockers called themselves "Bucca", a term which has a variety of meanings.

BUCCA, translated by Robert Morton Nance (c.1920) as "imp, hobgoblin, scarecrow", corresponds to the Irish "puca", the Welsh "pwca", and the English "puck". Originally, he would seem to have been a sea spirit, perhaps even the folk memory of an ancient sea-god, for whom fish from the catch were left on the shore in many ports. This practice carried on until quite late at MOUSEHOLE (SW 470265) and especially NEWLYN (SW 463290), where the foot of the steep Chywoone Hill is known as Bucca's Pass and, on the other side of the Newlyn River, a pinnacle of rock at Tolcarne is Bucca's Rock, where he has left the mark of his footprint and fishing net. Later legend made this the work of the Devil, but a local tradition was still remembered in Newlyn at the turn of the century of a troll-like being who lived in the rock and who foretold the future.

In ST IVES (SW 518405), a model boat called a "cock-dayka" was offered to the sea spirit – a tradition still remembered in the form of model boat sailing on the Consols Pool on Good Friday. This port also contained spirits which seem to form a link between Bucca and the Knockers; known as COOPERS, these made hammering noises in the cellars beneath the houses to foretell a catch of pilchards. Similar knockings made by the supernatural movement of pressing stones in the fish cellars had the same meaning.

The sea Bucca is normally described as a fish-eyed, leathery skinned being with hair like lank seaweed but his name also spread to ordinary ghosts. BUCCA WIDN ("white Bucca") was a benevolent spirit, whereas an evil one was BUCCA DUE ("black Bucca") and this name even came to mean the Devil.

Cornwall had other, minor forms of faery folk:

BROWNEY was also found in other areas of Britain. A helpful household spirit, Browney disappeared without trace when mechanisation came to the farms. Milk was always left at night for Browney, of whom no Cornish legends survive. There is, though, a curious reference from the 1880s when the Town Clerk of PENZANCE (SW 474303) reported that a respected gentlemen had told a local antiquarian meeting of a house close by where a Browney was still resident. The gentleman in question had often seen it sitting quietly by the fireside. For a long time, people would carefully tend their fireplaces, making sure the brandis was turned upside-down so that Browney wouldn't sit on it and burn himself, and, after cleaning the hearthstone, place a bowl of fresh water there for him to wash in.

THE HILLA and the STAG are creatures which give you a troublesome night. Never seen, they are described as great hairy creatures which sit on the sleeper's chest making breathing difficult. People suffering nightmares are still referred to as "hilla-ridden", and to "have the stag" is to suffer insomnia. If stabbed with an iron fork, they will instantly vanish for, like all faery folk, they are afraid of iron. It would appear that there is little difference between the two creatures except that the Hilla is responsible for bad dreams, while the Stag gives physical discomfort.

3

The Saints

Most of us were taught at school that it was St Augustine who converted Britain to Christianity in AD 597, but this, of course, is wrong. It was the Anglo-Saxons of Kent who were converted by him. Christianity had been present in Celtic Britain for at least 300 years, brought here during the Roman occupation, and in the year 314, these islands had a considerable Christian population in what is loosely described as the Celtic Church. The Christian word was spread by missionary monks such as Sucat, later known as St Patrick, a Briton from the Strathclyde area who did much to bolster the faith in Ireland (where Christian communities already existed).

Celtic monks from Wales and Ireland established a Christian southward trail, through Cornwall to the British colonies in Brittany, and it was these and a few Cornish-bred monks and priests who became the Cornish saints commemorated in so many of the Duchy's place-names. They were both men and women – having an equal standing in Celtic society – and the men at least wore their own form of the tonsure, shaving the front of the head from a line drawn from ear to ear.

Cornwall's "Age of the Saints" was from about AD 450 to AD 700 and many of the larger-than-life characters who founded church sites in Cornwall found themselves to be the very stuff of legend. As a result, stories about a number of the "Cornish Saints" survive.

ST AUSTOL, patrol of ST AUSTELL (SX 014524) and possibly a Breton, was the subject of a trick by the devil, who raised a wind to spin the saint around and blow his hat high into the air. The saint stuck his staff into the ground and trudged off to retrieve his hat, but found that the devil had transformed both hat and staff into stone. The Saint's (or Giant's) Hat, a huge round boulder, was destroyed by the military in 1798, but the staff – in reality – a Bronze Age menhir 11 feet tall, remained until its removal was made necessary by the extension of china-clay workings in the 1970s. It now stands or a green in the village of Roche (SW 986601). St Austol is said to have been the godson of St

Mewan (whose church stands only a mile away from Austol's). They were priests in the same Breton monastery and so attached that Austol died of grief only a week after Mewan's death.

The Longstone at Roche, said to have been St Austol's petrified staff (C. Weatherhill)

ST BERIANA whose church stands at ST BURYAN (SW 410258) is claimed to have been an Irish virgin whose powers of healing cured one of King Gerent of Cornwall's sons of paralysis.

ST BUDOC ("victor") has churches at BUDOCK (SW 786324), St Budeaux near Plymouth in Devon, and at Beuzec and Budamael in Brittany. The son of a Breton princess, St Azenor, he was born at sea after his mother had been sealed in a cask and flung into the sea. Miraculously preserved, mother and child survived a five-month journey from Brittany to Ireland. Both founded churches in Cornwall on their return to Brittany years later.

ST CLEDER, whose chapel and holy well stand in a beautiful valley at ST CLETHER (SX 203847) near the north-eastern edge of Bodmin Moor, is named as one of the Children of Brechan. There were 24 of these, men and women, who took instruction from their father, a Welsh chieftain of

Irish extraction (and after whom Brecon is named). Many of them came to Cornwall and an inscribed stone at St Endellion, bearing the Irish name BROCAGNUS, might even commemorate Brechan himself. It is most likely that the 24 saints were not actually the offspring of Brechan, but disciples who became known as his "children".

ST COLOM, the patron of ST COLUMB MAJOR (SW 912637) and MINOR (SW 839624), is thought by some to have been a man. In 1585, when the following legend was recorded, the saint was seen as a woman, COLUMBA. She fled from the attentions of her would-be "pagan lover" who decapitated her for refusing to renounce Christianity at Ruthvoes ("red wall").

ST COSTENTIN, name-saint of CONSTANTINE (SW 731291) was probably "Custennin Gorneu" ("Constantine of Cornwall"), a king of the south-western Celtic kingdom of Dumnonia which included Cornwall. Probably a son of Marc Cunomoros ("King Mark"), this 6th century king was railed by the monk Gildas as "the unclean whelp of the lioness of Dumnonia", but abdicated as an old man to enter a monastery before his death in 589.

ST DENNIS (SW 951583) was actually named after the hill fort ("dinas") in which it stands, but soon adopted St Denis, bishop of Paris. It is said that on the occasion of his execution at Monmartre (possibly in AD 258), blood fell on the stones of this Cornish churchyard. This occurred again when the great plague of 1665 broke out, and when Britain went to war with Holland.

ST ENDELIENT of ST ENDELLION (SW 997787) was one of the 24 Children of Brechan, and the Brocagnus Stone stands in her parish. She is said to have lived solely on the milk of a cow which strayed onto the land of the Lord of Trentinney. He killed the cow and, in turn, Endelient's godfather, King Arthur, slew him. The saint then miraculously restored him to life. Just before her death, Endelient asked that her body be placed on a cart to be drawn by year-old oxen and left to wander freely. Where they stopped became the site of her church.

ST GERENT, of the Roseland parish of GERRANS (SW 873352), was almost certainly another Dumnonian king, possibly the "Gerontios" to whom St Aldhelm, Abbot of Malmesbury, wrote in 705 of behalf of the Synod of Whitby, demanding that the Celtic Church conform to the doctrines of Rome. However it is more likely than the saint was an earlier king of the same name, who lived towards the end of the 6th century. Early genealogies state that two of his sons were Yestin (St Just) and Selyf (St Selevan, or St Levan). When Gerent died at his alleged castle of Dingerein, just outside Gerrans, his body was rowed across Veryan Bay in a golden ship with silver oars, to be buried under the great barrow of Carne Beacon, along with the fabulous ship. An earlier name for Dingerein ("Gerent's hill fort") was Cargurrel ("fort of the ship"), and a tunnel called the Mermaid's Hole is said to connect it to the cliffs.

ST GERMANUS, bishop of Auxerre in Gaul, visited Britain twice during the 5th century, in 429 and 446. Cornish tradition claims that he founded the first monastery at ST GERMANS (SX 360578). He actually died at Ravenna, Italy but local legend says that persecutors drove him from his church at St Germans.

Fearing for his life, he fled to Rame Head where his tears formed a holy well before a flaming chariot, driven by two angels, descended. They told him to curse his persecutors and from that time all holiness left the church he had built. The angels transported him to other lands to continue his calling.

The chapel on Rame Head marks the spot where St Germanus was carried off by an angelic chariot (P. Devereux)

ST GWINEAR, the Cornish form of the Irish Fionngar, has his church inland from St Ives Bay (SW 596374). He is said to have been the leader of a band of Irish Christian settlers who landed in the bay at the mouth of the Hayle River. There, they fell foul of the local tyrant king Teudar who massacred them. After being beheaded, Gwinear picked up his head and walked inland to the site of the present church. Where he planted his staff at Roseworthy, his holy well sprang up. Gwinear's sister Piala, who also died in the massacre, has her church on a creek of the Hayle estuary at Phillack (now dedicated to St Felicitas).

ST IA (pronounced "eea") also sailed from Ireland to St Ives Bay at the same time as Gwinear and his ill-fated party. She, however, had a very different reception. Landing at St Ives (SW 518405), she had a chapel built for her by another local chieftain named Dinan. In legend, St Ia sailed across the Celtic Sea on a leaf, this suggesting that her craft may actually have been a traditional Irish curragh.

ST JUST has churches in the far west of Cornwall (SW 372315) and in a beautiful creekside spot in the Roseland peninsula (SW 848357). He is believed by many to have been Yestin, son of King Gerent, who is strongly connected with the Roseland, and brother of Selyf or Selevan (see ST LEVAN). Legend isn't kind to St Just; in his western parish he was said to have a perpetual feud with neighbouring St Senan (Sennen).

Another story tells of St Just's visit to St Keverne on the Lizard peninsula, and making off with Keverne's favourite chalice. Keverne pursued him, picked up three great gabbro boulders from Crousa Downs and flung them at the fleeing chief. They missed but Just dropped the chalice and made his get-away. The "Try-mean-Keverne" (three stones of Keverne) lay by the roadside between Breage and Germoe until the turn of the century when they were broken up for roadstone. St Just's name became East (pron. "ai-est") in Cornish, so that in his western parish Venton East is St Just's Well, and Priest Cove was originally Por East, St Just's Cove.

ST KEA was a British bishop who founded a creekside church on the upper reaches of the Fal estuary. At Old Kea (SW 844417) the tower of the medieval church remains. A new church site was founded at Kea (SW 810427) in 1802. St Kea went on to found a monastery at Cleder in Brittany. Legend says that he returned to Britain just once; to attempt a mediation between King Arthur and Mordred. He may originally have been a Glastonbury monk.

St LEVAN, properly Selevan which some claim to be a Cornish form of Solomon. He is said to have been Selyf, brother of St Just, son of King Gerent and father of St Kyby (Cuby). His church is situated in a valley on the coast near Land's End (SW 381223), at the foot of which is the cove of Chapel Porth, formerly Porth Selevan. Here, on the clifftop stands his holy well, from which a flight of ancient steps descends to a ledge and the remains of the saint's chapel and cell. A number of stories survive about St Levan. A local woman called Johanna, while tending her garden, spotted the saint on his way to do a spot of fishing on a Sunday, and rebuked him for doing so on the Sabbath. he replied that fishing was no worse than gardening and declared that any future child of the parish to be called Johanna would grow to be a big a fool as she.

The Selus Stone in St Just church may have marked the grave of St Levan (Selevan), reputedly St Just's brother (C. Weatherhill)

Since then, no child of St Levan parish has been christened Johanna. St Leven was said to have lived for a while at Bodellan in the Porthcurno valley and the path from there, past Rospletha to the church site and on to the cove is still a footpath. Another story is that this fisherman priest caught two chad on the same hook. He threw them back, but again and again they returned to the hook. In the end he took them home and served them to his sister's children. They choked on the bones and since then, the chad has been called "chuck-cheel" (choke-child). In this way, an apparent blessing became a curse. In the churchyard is a rounded earthfast boulder, split through the middle. Almost certainly a pre-Christian sacred rock, St Levan's Stone was split by a blow from the saint's fist and he (or some say, Merlin) uttered the prophecy that: "When, with panniers astride, a pack-horse can ride, Through St Levan's Stone, the world will be done". There is no need to worry quite yet.

ST MERIASEK has his church at Camborne (SW 644400). A medieval Cornish miracle play, "Beunans Meriasek" (Life of Meriasek), held that he came from Brittany. On settling in Cornwall, he confronted the infamous King Teudar in arguments about Christianity. Teudar plotted to rid himself of this troublesome priest but Meriasek was warned, avoided the king by hiding under the rock called Carack Veriasek (not known today, but evidently was in 1504 when the play was written) and escaping back to Brittany where he later became Bishop of Vannes.

ST MINVER's church is in North Cornwall (SW 965771). A Christian priestess, she was set upon by Satan while combing her hair. She flung the sharp-toothed comb at him with deadly accuracy and the arch-field fled.

ST NECTAN, eldest of the Children of Brechan, did not found a parish, although he was honoured at Hartland Abbey and had a chapel dedicated to him near Lostwithiel. His most sacred Cornish site, though, is the beautiful 20 metre waterfall in the wooded ravine of St Nectan's Glen near Tintagel (SX 081885), where, on a pinnacle of rock above the falls, he founded a chapel. In the tower of this chapel he hung a silver bell and, when on his death-bed, he told his followers that the bell would keep the light of Christ alive. At his request, they carried him on a litter to a ledge above St Nectan's Kieve, a great, smooth-sided cauldron of rock into which the water falls before flowing out and falling again through a natural arch. The saint dropped the bell into the clear waters of the Kieve, where it vanished from sight. When he died, two foreign women took over this chapel and placed the body of the saint and all his treasures into a great oak chest. They then turned the river aside, buried the chest, and let the river revert to its course to flow forever over the saint's grave. The women continued to live at the chapel as recluses until one died, closely followed by the other. Their grave is said to be under a great flat slab near the foot of the falls. Centuries later, a group of quarrymen resolved to find the silver bell by blasting the Kieve. They were about to set the charges when they heard the clear sound of the bell and voice proclaiming that: "The child is not yet born who shall recover this treasure". The operation ceased and was never resumed.

The beautiful waterfall at St Nectan's Kieve, a deeply sacred spot (P. Devereux)

ST NEOT has his church in a beautiful wooded valley setting (SX 187679), on a site which was originally the shrine of St Guerir. Neot, a Glastonbury monk who journeyed west to Cornwall, is traditionally related to King Alfred. Other traditions state that he was a dwarf, not more than 15 inches tall. Unusually devout, St Neot was said to stand up to his neck in the cold water of the nearby holy well while he recited the entire Book of Psalms. Four tales of St Neot link him closely with animals and it would seem that he is a local St Francis of Assisi. In one, a hunted fox devours one of Neot's shoes but is found, in an exhausted state, with the thongs hanging from his mouth. The intact shoe is drawn out and returned to the saint. On another occasion, a hunted doe fled to the saint's protection. The pursuing hounds were halted in their tracks by the saint's commanding gaze, as was a huntsman poised to loose an arrow into the doe's heart. From that day on, the huntsman became a follower of St Neot, even presenting him with his hunting horn which hung in the church for many years afterwards. A third story relates that, with seeding time running short and the church fields in urgent need of ploughing, thieves stole Neot's plough-oxen. The saint was undaunted and, at his call, wild stags came out of the forest to willingly lend their necks to the yoke. On hearing of this, the thieves relented, returned the oxen and became monks. The released stags forever bore a white ring, like a yoke, around their necks, and enjoyed divine protection from the hunters. The fourth tale relates that Neot received the divine gift of three fish in his well, but he was only to catch one each day. If this was obeyed, he would find that, on the next morning, the well contained three fish again. Unfortunately, the saint fell ill and his servant Barius went to the well on his behalf, catching two of the fish. One of these he boiled, the other he broiled. Aghast, Neot prayed over the cooked fish and commanded Barius to return them to the well. He did so and, as each entered the water, they were miraculously restored to life. Elements from these stories are depicted in the windows of the church. After Neot died, his spirit appeared to the shrine guardian, commanding him to remove his remains to St Neots, Cambridgeshire.

ST PERRAN has supplanted St Petroc and St Michael as Cornwall's patron saint and it is his flag – the white cross on a black background – which flies on the 5th March, St Perran's Day. His name has been given to three Cornish parishes; Perranzabuloe (SW 770520), Perranarworthal (SW 779389), and Perranuthnoe (SW 538295), as well as the 19th century seaside town of Perranporth (SW 756544) and a holy well in the parish of

Probus, Venton Berran (SW 867477). Perran is unlikely to have been the Ciaran of Saighir cited by many in the past; he was probably a British priest and is also found in Brittany at Trezelide. Connected with his Irish tradition is the tale that Perran was chained to a millstone and cast from a clifftop in Ireland. Miraculously, the millstone floated and bore Perran to Cornwall, where he built his oratory in the sand-dunes north of Perranporth. He is said to have discovered tin, or, more likely, an improved method of smelting, and the celebrations were so intense that they originated the saying "drunk as a Perraner". In the mid 18th century, the miners of Breage and Germoe adopted him as their patron saint, and this practice soon spread to all Cornish miners. He is often found as St Piran, but Perran is a more correct spelling of his name.

ST PETROC was believed to have come from South Wales, landing in the Camel estuary at Trebetherick and founding the great monastic centre at Padstow (SW 916754), later superceded by the priority at Bodmin. He came across religious sceptics who were convinced when he created a holy well by rapping his staff on the ground, causing water to flow. Petroc went on to Brittany and on a pilgrimage to Rome and Jerusalem. It is even claimed that he lived for a while as a hermit on an island in the Indian Ocean. Eventually he returned to Cornwall where he removed the troublesome ghost of Jan Tregeagle, helped a dragon with a splinter in its eye and, like St Neot, sheltering a hunted doe and converting the huntsmen, Constantine, and his followers. Petroc's relics were kept at his foundation at Bodmin until 1177, when they were stolen and taken to the Breton church of St Meen. They were restored by order of King Henry II. For a while, Petroc vied for the position of Cornwall's patron saint.

ST SANCRET gave his name to the western parish of Sancreed (SW 421294), though some call him St Credan. He is alleged to have accidentally killed his father and, in penance, took to a life as a hermit and swineherd, hence the nickname of Sancreed parishioners: "Sancreed Pigs".

ST SENARA is the patron of Zennor (SW 454385) and may have been the Breton princess Azenor, daughter of King Hoel II, who was falsely accused of adultery by her husband's jealous stepmother. Her punishment was to be nailed into a cask and flung into the sea. Fed by an angel, she survived the ordeal of a five-month voyage, even giving birth to her son Budec on the way. She landed in Ireland, where she remained for many years. The truth of her innocence was confessed by the stepmother on her deathbed, and the horrified husband called Azenor home. On the way, she stopped off in Cornwall, where she founded Zennor, and her son, the church at Budock near Falmouth. There are a number of legends of holy women from the sea on this coast and Zennor is most famous for its mermaid. Can it be that " St Senara" is a Christianised memory of an ancient sea-goddess?

The holy well and chapel of St Sancret (C. Weatherhill)

ST WYLLOC, is also known as St Willow, is commemorated at Lanteglos-by-Fowey (SX 144515). Apparently Irish in origin, he was slain at Lamellyn in his Cornish parish by his own brother, Melin. Although beheaded, Wylloc, like St Gwinear, picked up his head and carried it to the later chapel site nearby before expiring.

4

Church Legends

Most Cornish churches have extremely ancient origins. The 14th and 15th century structures seen today often stand on the site of Norman churches, many of which had replaced early Celtic foundations. In many cases, the Celtic churches had been set up on pre-Christian ceremonial or occupation sites. Quite recently, the raised oval "lan" surrounding ST BURYAN church (SW 400258) was found to have developed from an Iron Age enclosure.

In early times, Christianity struggled to overcome the beliefs of the pagan Celts whose gods and goddesses became, in Christian eyes, synonymous with the devil that had to be overcome. It could not have been easy for the early priests and monks to establish their churches on revered pagan sites, and the record of their struggle is reflected by the tales of the devil making life difficult for the church builders.

The devil had a particular dislike for the church towers, chiefly because they contained the bells he could not bear to hear. At EGLOSH-AYLE church (SX 001719), beside the Camel river, he is said to have flung a stone at the tower as it was being built.

TOWEDNACK church (SW 487381), in a secluded and lonely spot on the Penwith moors, has a squat tower which, unusually for churches in West Cornwall, has no corner pinnacles. These were intended in the design but as the builders set them up by day, so the devil tore them down by night. Eventually the builders gave up and outside the church porch is one of the original pinnacles, now surmounted by an ancient stone cross. A local saying holds that: "There are no cuckolds in Towednack parish because there are no horns on the church tower", the logic of which escapes me.

PROBUS church (SW 899477) has Cornwall's tallest and most ornately carved church tower. This was intended for Truro, five miles away, but the devil upset the cart in which the tower was being carried – in one piece! – at Probus, and so it was erected where it fell.

In the extreme south-west of the Duchy, ST LEVAN church (SW

381222) was to have been built at Raftra, at the head of the valley, but as the stones were brought to the Raftra site, so they were spirited away to the present site by night.

At LUDGVAN (SW 505331), it was either the devil or a lesser demon who, after being exorcised from Treassowe House, to the north-west of the village, entered a local child. It took a further bout of exorcism to banish the demon who, before departing for the Red Sea (the usual place of demonic exile), snapped a pinnacle from the church tower and spat in the holy well, so destroying its power to cure diseases of the eye (but not its protection against hanging). An interesting footnote to this is that an upturned granite trough at Treassowe was believed to have entrapped a spirit exorcised by Parson John Stephens, but the trough was later righted, freeing the troublesome spirit. The church tower was indeed damaged, by a thunderstorm in July 1761, but Stephens did not become Rector of the parish until thirty years later.

LADOCK church (SW 894510) experienced a period when its bells were out of order. They could not be serviced due to the presence of a demon in the shape of a great black bird which constantly perched on the church tower, terrifying churchgoers and emitting hideous noises during the services. The Rector was Parson Woods, another noted exorcist, who carried an ebony walking stick with a pentacle engraved on its silver knob and mystic signs on a broad silver band below the knob. His technique usually consisted of changing demons and spirits into animal form and thrashing them with his whip. However, this demon was well out of reach of the Rector's whip, so he devised another method of exorcism. No demon can endure the sight of innocent children and Woods arranged for twelve babies to be brought to the church. This number, the same as that of the apostles, would render the action particularly powerful. Four of these were already baptised and Woods christened the others there and then before holding each up to show to the demon. The great bird refused to look, preferring to hide behind one of the pinnacles. Then, one of the children began to cry, so setting the other eleven off as well. The sudden din caused the demon to look down from the tower, only to find himself staring at twelve innocent and lustily bawling children. Letting-out an earthly screech, he flew from the tower, never to return.

A more benevolent power was responsible for the siting of TALLAND church (SX 228516). The chosen site was well inland at a place called Pulpit, but the stones laid by day were mysteriously moved at night to the site of the present church. An unexplained voice informed the builders that: "If you would my wish fulfil; Build my church on Talland Hill".

The church tower at MINSTER (SX 111905) is incomplete and finished off with a saddleback roof. According to legend it was once much higher and carried a light to guide pilgrims. Fishermen hated it. Being visible from the sea at the end of Boscastle's ravine-like harbour, it constantly misled them, sometimes with tragic consequences. Enraged, the seamen pulled down the tower, which was never rebuilt.

Blight's drawing of Minster church

Close by stands FORRABURY church (SX 096909), whose tower contains no bells at all. A fine set was once ordered, made, and sent by ship to Boscastle harbour. As the ship approached, the bells of Tintagel church rang out and the pilot voiced his thanks to God for the fair wind and safe voyage. The captain retorted that it had nothing to do with God; they should thank themselves, and especially the captain, for their fine seamanship. At that moment, a huge and inexplicable wave swamped the ship, sending it and the Forrabury bells to the bottom of the sea. Only the devout pilot was saved. The ringing of the submerged bells foretell a storm, and the tower has been silent from that day to this.

ST ANTHONY IN ROSELAND church (SW 855320) has a maritime origin. Shortly after the Norman Conquest, noblemen were crossing the Channel from Normandy when they were overtaken by a violent storm. They prayed to St Anthony and vowed to erect a church in his honour at their place of landing, if they avoided shipwreck. The storm blew them into the safety of the Fal estuary and the mouth of the Percuil river where the church now stands.

In the Rame peninsula of South-east Cornwall, SHEVIOCK church (SX 370551) was reputedly built by the powerful Sir John de Daunay who planned a fine, large building but decided at the last to cut his costs and limit its size. His wife, Lady Emelyn, was appalled by this and resolved to shame him by building a barn close by which would be more beautiful than the developing church. It is said that the devil aided her, and that the barn grew with unnatural speed. Indeed, it was superior to the church in every way.

A 15th century legend of the building of the church on ST MICHAEL'S MOUNT (SW 515299) tells that: "there were two rocks, one on either side of the church, so that the work could not be carried higher because of them. St Michael bade a man, one night, to go thither and put away these rocks and fear nothing. Then this man went thither and set his shoulder to the rocks and bade them in the name of God and St Michael to move outward, and so they did as much as was the need".

Many people feared to be buried on the north side of a church, where the sun would not shine on the grave, and at least one vicar threatened this fate to a parishioner with whom he'd fallen out. This was one James Hosking of Treassowe, Ludgvan, who, after such a threat, constructed his own walled burial plot high on the hill of CASTLE-AN-DINAS (SW 485350). Into its walls he placed plaques declaring that: "Custom is the idol of fools" and "Virtue only consecrates the ground". The burial plot, with the bodies of Hosking and two of his children, is no longer on the hill – in its place is a huge quarry. The reinterred remains lie at a ruined chapel at Shillingham Manor, Saltash, owned by Hosking's descendants.

5

Legends of the Mines

It is not altogether surprising that many strange beliefs gathered around Cornwall's world-famous tin and copper mines. These two metals in particular have been extracted from Cornish ground from prehistoric times and possibly as far back as 2000 BC, when bronze, an alloy of tin and copper, was in demand throughout Europe.

The tinfields of West Cornwall were visited c.300 BC by the Massalia (Marseilles) based Greek explorer and geographer Pytheas, and commented upon 200 years later by Diodorus of Sicily, probably quoting from Pytheas' lost texts. From those days until the 17th century, tin-mining in Cornwall consisted of streaming – extensive excavations in tin-bearing valley gravels – and lodeback digging, where the lodes outcropped on the surface. Deep mining could not be considered until the problem of pumping could be properly addressed. Mechanical horse-whims, which drew from shallow shafts were eventually superceded by the power of the steam engine and, in the 18th and 19th centuries, Cornish ingenuity came to the fore, arguably leading the way in the Industrial Revolution through the works of Richard Trevithick, Goldsworthy Gurney, Sir Humphry Davy and others. Shafts could now be sunk to great depths – Cornwall's deepest shaft is 1,000 metres deep – and coastal mines such as those in the western parish of St Just were often driven out under the sea. Some levels were so close to the sea-bed that miners could clearly hear the boulders rolling around above their heads.

The miners themselves worked incredibly hard for little reward, and the rich mine owners were not best known for taking an interest in the welfare and safety of those whose dangerous work made them rich. Such is the truth of the Cornish mines and their "romantic" remains of crumbling granite engine houses and dressing floors. Accidents and disasters were commonplace: it was a managerial mistake which caused the miners of Wheal Owles to hole into the flooded workings of Wheal Drea in January 1893, resulting in the horrific deaths of 19 miners, all of whom remain in the inundated depths of the mine to this day. The 20th century saw massive improvements in working standards and rewards but few mines remained in work. Now, only South Crofty Mine at Camborne remains in production.

19th century engraving of Botallack Mine, whose workings run out under the sea.

It is only natural that workers in this dark, alien environment, constantly rubbing shoulders with death, should form beliefs and taboos of their own. In Chapter 2 of this book, we met the sprites of the Cornish mines, the Knockers, who continue to work the hundreds of mines abandoned for economic rather than geological reasons. After all, it is said with some truth that "there is more tin in Cornwall than was ever taken out of it".

The activities of Knockers are recorded in a number of mines, chiefly in the Land's End peninsula: BALLOWALL MINE, St Just (SW 357313), BALLESWIDDEN (SW 389312), also near St Just, and the ROSEWALL & RANSOM MINES, St Ives (SW 497392), in particular.

Other mines contained different supernatural inhabitants. At WHEAL VOR (SW 620300), a once extensive and rich mine near Breage, a forewarning of fatal accidents in the mine appeared in the form of a white hare or rabbit. Usually, this represents the ghost of a woman who has lost her life through being betrayed in love but no such origin is recalled for the apparition at Wheal Vor, where it normally appeared above ground in one of the engine houses. Miners had been known to chase the white hare into corners and stopped-up pipes but always it escaped without explanation.

In the early 19th century, a man and a boy were sinking a shaft at Wheal Vor when, through some mishap, a charge of explosives blew up prematurely, shattering their bodies so horrifically that they were unrecognisable. When the remains were brought up to the surface, the clothes and a lump of mangled flesh dropped from the bodies to be hastily whipped up by an onlooker's shovel and tossed into the nearly furnace of Woolf's engine. From that time on, troops of small black dogs haunted the place and it soon became hard to find anyone willing to work the engine.

WHEAL JEWELL (SW 734421) developed a chilling phantom of its own, following the death of a miner who fell while ascending the ladders in one of its shafts. For a brief while, his spectral form was occasionally seen at surface before manifesting itself in a different way. The district began to speak with horror of "the dead hand". This was seen moving up and down the shaft; a disembodied hand holding a ball of clay, in which was set a lighted candle. The clay was held between thumb and forefinger, while the other fingers grasped successive rungs of the ladder. Many believed that sight of the dead hand would trigger misfortune upon any who witnessed it.

John Lean, a member of a rich mining family, encountered another supernatural presence in Wheal Jewell. While examining a rich lode in the depths of the mine, he suddenly heard a clear voice exclaim: "You are in the winze"! Knowing that he was alone, Lean flung himself over onto his back before discovering that he had been inches from the edge of a deep pit into which he would have fallen to his death had he not been warned.

In Cornwall's deepest 19th century mine, DOLCOATH (SW 658404) at Camborne, eight men who were trapped underground by a rock fall and later rescued owed their lives to ghostly cracklings in the rock which scared them into moving away, thereby avoiding the rockfall.

POLBREEN MINE (SW 719504) lies under the village of St Agnes. Here the tale is told of a woman called Anne Dorcas who tired of life and threw herself into one of the mine's deep shafts. After her body had been recovered and buried, her presence continued to haunt the mine. Miners found themselves being lured away from their work by a voice calling their names, and tributers, miners who worked for a share of the profits in lieu of wages, who had a poor production month were asked if they had been "chasing Dorcas". The ghost generally took the form of a voice and delighted in making mischief. Sometimes it would manifest itself enough to tear the clothes from a miner's back but there was one occasion where Dorcas acted in mercy. Two miners working deep in Polbreen heard one of their names being repeatedly called. In exasperation, the miner concerned dropped his tools and went to investigate. No sooner had he moved away than a huge portion of the roof collapsed without warning onto the very spot where he had stood. His companion was trapped but unhurt, and was soon dug out. To his dying day, the miner whose name had been called swore that he owed his life to Dorcas. Dorcas's Shaft – sometimes corrupted to Darkey's Shaft and where the unhappy woman had thrown herself to her death – lies in a neglected plot on the south side of the car park off Trelawney Road in St Agnes. it is poorly capped and should not be approached.

In a mine near ST AUSTELL a miner was killed by a rock fall. Some time later, another miner was working near the fatal spot when he saw a cloud of smoke form above the floor of the level and begin to assume the shape of his dead colleague. In horror he fell back and, at that moment, part of the roof fell on the spot where he had stood.

Even those miners who left Cornwall to find work in hard-rock mining abroad could not escape their ghosts. One Cornishman, working at a mine in Pachuca, Mexico, dreamed one night of his daughter who had stayed in Cornwall. He dreamed that she laid a cold hand on his brow, saying sadly: "Oh, father"! He later learned that she had died that very night.

Cornish miners always spoke reverently of "the old men", those miners of the distant past. Ancient streaming sites and lodeback excavations were referred to as "old men's workings". There was a belief, only slightly supported by history, that Jews had once been employed in Cornish mines. Old smelting sites were "Jew's Houses", and, to some, the Knockers were the spirits of Jews who had encouraged the crucifixion of Christ and who had been divinely sentenced to hard labour in Cornwall's dark and dripping mines. Part of their penance was to observe, and therefore not work, on the Christian festivals of Christmas,

An atmospheric engine house at Ding Dong Mine (C. Weatherhill)

Easter, and All Saints' Day, although a concession was made that they should also not work on Saturdays, the Jewish Sabbath. At Christmas, they were compelled to sing carols deep in the mines. This train of belief seems to stem from the rampant anti-Semitism of King John's reign and it is said that John himself sent Jewish prisoners to work in Cornwall's mines.

The name "Market Jew", sometimes given to Marazion and also naming the main shopping street of Penzance leading to Marazion, has nothing to do with Jewish people at all: it is the Late Cornish "Marhas Jeu" (Thursday market).

Nor does the continuing story of Phoenician traders sailing here for Cornish tin have any real credence. The concept was dreamed up by a 16th century schoolmaster named John Twynne, and was such an attractive idea that it caught on and is still quoted as "fact", even though archaeology cannot find a shred of evidence to support it. Even those ancient commentators Pytheas and Diodorus Siculus make it clear that Cornish tin was shipped to what is now Brittany, and then overland to Massalia. Nevertheless, there are beliefs that DING DONG MINE (SW 438348) was visited by Joseph of Arimathea, and even the young Christ himself. Ding Dong is undoubtedly a very old mine with possible prehistoric origins and, in local belief, the streamworks in TREWEY BOTTOMS (SW 463375) near Zennor, and the cliff mine of BAL-LOWALL, St Just, were "worked before the Flood". Evidence of tin-smelting was turned up in the Iron Age fort of CHUN CASTLE (SW 405339), which legend held had been built by Jack of the Hammer, or Jack the Tinner – now seen as an embodiment of the multi-skilled Celtic god Lugh.

The hardened miners of Cornwall, whose unparalleled expertise in hard-rock mining has been spread as far afield as Australia, the United States, Mexico, Bolivia, Peru and South Africa, had a series of strict taboos. Like the coal miners of Wales and Northumbria, whistling was banned underground, with one old miner recalling that the first thing he was told before he ever went below grass was "that I should have me skull bate in if I 'cocked lip' (whistled) under adit level".

Also banned from underground was the making of the sign of the cross. One man who marked his path in the labyrinth of a Cornish mine with chalk crosses was told in no uncertain manner to change them.

Animals and birds were never to be named. Instead, the miners concocted nicknames by which they could be mentioned without harm.

The fox was "long tail" (which equates with its nickname in the Cornish language: "lostack"); and the owl was given the grand alternative title of "braced farcer". Cats were "rookers", hares "long ear" (again this parallels the Cornish "scovarnack" for a hare), and rats "peeps".

Carn Galva Mine (P. Devereux)

The high-pitched shrieks of rats were said to warn of rock-falls, even though rats are seldom found in mine workings. Toads were held to be propitious and the humble snail found itself the object of great respect. If a miner passed one on his way to work, he would stop and leave a piece of his candle tallow by its side as an offering to guard against accidents in the mine. Spiders were believed to be the bringers of good luck if they happened to alight upon the face or shoulder.

A fragment of the miners' lunch, usually the 'hoggan' (pasty) or "fuggan" (heavy cake), would always be left for the Knockers and, if a miner found he had forgotten something before going underground, he would not return for the item, whatever it was, or, if he did, he would not then go back to the mine until the next day: "Forget, return and there remain; Or bad luck follows in thy train".

It cannot be stressed too highly that Cornwall's mining sites must be treated with the greatest respect. They are very dangerous places and the best advice is that any visitor to these sites should not stray from clearly worn paths. Many shafts are unprotected and even some of those which are capped, particularly in mid-Cornwall where the very dubious 'Clwyd Cap' (which resembles a child's climbing frame) was extensively and ill-advisedly used in the 1980s, should be avoided for safety's sake. A few of the engine houses have been consolidated in recent years, but most have not. In many cases, these are crumbling and should be viewed as potentially dangerous. Please take the greatest care.

6

Mystery Lights

In folklore throughout the world, there is often mention of weird lights, which are frequently interpreted in differing contexts. The rich lore of Cornwall is no exception, as we can soon see if we look at some examples.

In Cornwall, as in all Celtic lands, strange lights are traditionally seen as *faeries* – literally "faery lights". That uniquely Cornish spirit, the Piskey, for instance, was often considered an unsociable sprite, who enjoyed leading people into bogs by appearing as an inviting light ahead in the dark night, like a welcoming glow from a distant cottage window, or from a lantern. There is an east Cornish rhyme relating to this:

Jack o'the lantern! Joan the Wad,
Who tickled the maid and made her mad;
Light me home, the weather's bad.

THE GUMP, that stretch of moorland around the northeast of Carn Kenidjack (SW 388330), figures repeatedly in Cornish lore as a haunt of the faeries. It was associated with mysterious lights. Hunt passes on one story concerning a greedy fellow who went out onto the Gump during the harvest moon in order to seize the fairy treasure that was bound to be there. He had not gone far, when he heard beautiful, enchanting music, coming from beneath the ground. Keeping his wits sharp, he lay in wait. Suddenly, a hillock or mound before him opened up, and all around him was ablaze with multi-coloured lights. The entranced man then saw a troop of small people emerge from their subterranean haunt, playing on every kind of instrument. They arranged themselves on the ground in such a way that the spot where he hid was surrounded. A further crowd of small beings brought out rich jewellery and silver and gold vessels, then the lights intensified in brilliance and there appeared countless beautiful small creatures dressed in exquisite finery. The Gump was alive with glittering lights and faery splendour. So fixed was the greedy man's attention on all this, he failed to note that the first lot of beings had thrown a web of threads around him, the ends of which they held. the man crept cautiously towards the glittering array of lights in front of the mound, but suddenly the alarm went up from the faery host, and the fellow found himself enmeshed by the faery threads as the little sprites buzzed around him like flies. As the sun rose, the man found himself alone on the moor, tied to the ground by thousands of gossamer webs, glistening with dew ...

J.T. Blight's atmospheric rendering of Carn Kenidjack

Another tale associated with the Gump tells of a strange gleaming light on the rocks of Carn Kenidjack seen by two miners on their way home from the now abandoned mines at Morvah. They went on to have an unnerving adventure featuring a dark horseman, perhaps the Devil himself! (See Chapter 9.)

Borlase noted in 1885 that miners returning from work at night sometimes reported seeing lights burning on the Neolithic BALLOWALL BARROW (NG 356312), or Carn Gluze or Gloose, on the clifftops near St Just. These were of course interpreted as faeries, as were lights seen occasionally next to the LOGAN ROCK (SW 397220) on the headland beyond Treryn Dinas cliff castle near Porthcurno. Regarding these, an old resident of the area told Hunt: "On a fine summer's night, I have heard the sweetest of music, and seen hundreds of little lights moving about".

Mystery lights were oftentimes taken as omens. The miners dreaded seeing the "Dead Hand". A small light with irregular motion seen in a shaft was taken to be the flame of a candle held in the disembodied, spectral hand of a miner killed in some former accident (see previous chapter for the classic account of this at Wheal Jewell). To see this light was to forewarn of disaster.

Ballowall Barrow (Carn Gloose), situated on sea cliffs over mineral ores and mine workings, where miners saw 'faery lights' (P. Devereux)

The "Lady and the Lantern" at St Ives was an omen for the fishermen. If the light was seen flitting over the rocks which lead out to the sea from the eastern side of "The Island" or ST IVES HEAD (SW 522412) it was taken as a sure warning of an impending disaster along that length of coast. The legend attached to the light concerns a fierce storm along that seashore which caused a ship to be in terrible peril. The brave fishermen of St Ives put out at dusk in the teeth of the storm to save the souls aboard the vessel. Although all efforts to save the ship failed, the fishermen managed to get a woman and baby off the stricken vessel, but as she was being hauled to the fisherman's boat the woman fainted and let the child slip into the raging sea. The woman recovered later on shore, but died shortly afterwards of a broken heart at losing her child. Her ghost was said to search the rocks for her baby, and on stormy nights she carried a lantern to help her in her doomed task.

Treryn (Treen) Dinas cliff-castle, where swarms of 'faery lights' were seen from time to time (P. Devereux)

Another prophetic light phenomenon in the folklore is "Jack Harry's lights", which supposedly herald a storm. They are said to form on a phantom vessel resembling the one that will be lost during the storm.

Chains of a strange fire used to be seen ascending and descending over TREVILLEY CLIFF (SW 350238) near Land's End, and this was said to forewarn of the death of a member of a family that used to live in the district.

Trevilley Cliff (the far headland, with caves). A mythic spot recurring in Cornish folklore, and where strange flickering columns of light used to be seen (P. Devereux)

Not far along that piece of coastline is TOL-PEDN-PENWITH where the cliff called Chair Ladder is situated (at SW 365216). This, we will learn in Chapter 8, was where the old witch, Madge Figgy used to go to summon up storms (and from where she was said to fly off into the night on a stem of ragwort). On one occasion, it is said that Madge lured a rich Portuguese ship into Por Loe (Porth Loe or Perloe Cove). All the passengers were drowned, and Madge and her wrecking party stripped the washed-up bodies of their jewels and finery. But Madge forbade anyone to touch the body of a richly-dressed and bejewelled woman; the witch saw a mark on the dead woman which meant evil for anyone touching it. With caution, Madge buried the body and stored the clothing and jewellery in a chest which she kept in her but at Raftra. That night, a light arose from the woman's grave on the clifftop, and passed along the cliffs to Chair Ladder where it stayed for several hours. Then it moved off and passed over the country to Madge's hut, where it settled on the chest. This occurrence took place each night for three months. Then a foreign stranger arrived in St Levan and by sign language asked the way to the shipwreck victims' graves at Por Loe. There he immediately picked out the grave of the dead woman and gave vent to his grief. He awaited the appearance of the light that night, then followed it all the way to Madge Figgy's hut. There, he opened the chest and removed the woman's jewellery but refused to take any of the other valuables there. He rewarded the wreckers with costly gifts and left. As Madge said: "One witch knows another witch, dead or living, and the African would have been the death of us if we hadn't kept the treasure, whereas we now have good gifts and no gainsaying them".

Porth Loe (P. Devereux)

Cornish churches and chapels do not escape association with mystery lights. Again, the traditional reference is with regard to faeries. For instance, the church of LELANT (SW 548378), in the sandhills near the entrance to the creek at Hayle, was said to be used by the faeries. The tales tell of a man returning one evening from St Ives, where he had bought some fish, when he saw lights in LELANT church. He approached more closely and looked in: at first he saw just a general illumination, but gradually perceived a fairy funeral taking place!

But modern eyewitness accounts also tell of similar things, albeit shorn of faery connotations. In one case at BOSSINEY (SW 078894), author and publisher Michael Williams, with friends, saw a light in the windows of the Methodist chapel there. This building stands close to Bossiney Mound, said in lore to contain King Arthur's Round Table (Tintagel is close by) which rises to the surface of the mound surrounded by shimmering light on Midsummer's Eve. Williams and friends were lightheartedly testing this old legend when they in fact saw "a flow rather than a single shaft of electricity – like a patch of floodlit moorland mist" appear inside one of the chapel's windows. Soon the glow could be seen at two windows. The phenomenon lasted only a minute or so. The witnesses checked the chapel: it was dark and empty inside, and, moreover, there were blinds on the two windows concerned!

Interestingly, a letter dated 1 December 1858, appeared in *The Times* on 4 December, 1858, described a mystery light seen near BOSTCASTLE (SW 099908), only a few miles along the north Cornish coast from Bossiney:

> Last night, at 15 minutes to 9, it being very dark and raining heavily, I was ascending one of the steep hills of this neighbourhood, when suddenly I was surrounded by a bright and powerful light, which passed me a little quicker than the ordinary pace of man's walking, leaving it dark as before.
>
> This day I have been informed that the light was seen by the sailors in the harbour, coming in from the sea and passing up the valley like a low cloud.

This relatively modern eyewitness account contains intriguing echoes of a most curious legend associated with SENNEN COVE (SW 355265) on the western tip of Cornwall, close by Land's End. This involves a "spirit" which was known as "The Hooper". It was described by W. Bottrell as "a compact cloud of mist" which would appear even when the weather "was by no means foggy". It would stop over Cowloe rocks in Whitesand Bay at Sennen Cove, then spread like a dense, misty cloud right across the local coastline. At night, a dull light was seen within the mist, with sparks flaring upwards as if a fire was concealed within the vapour. At the same time, "hooping" sounds were heard from the phenomenon. It was believed that the mist shrouded a spirit that came to forewarn of approaching storms, and those who nevertheless put to sea regardless found a kind of resistance from the within the eerie fog. The story goes that a reckless fisherman and his son literally beat their way through the supernatural fog with a flail, but were never seen again, and the Hooper never returned.

In *Notes and Queries* of 16th December, 1865, there was a report of a recurring light phenomenon at ST AUSTELL. It appeared almost nightly at Hillhead, to the west of the town, particularly in November and December. The correspondent referred to an entry in *Gentleman's Magazine* of 1827 which described the light thus:

> It appears of a yellow hue, and seems to resemble a small flame. It is generally stationary, and when it moves it wanders but little from its primitive spot, sometimes mounting upward, and then descending to the earth. As it has frequented this spot from time immemorial, it is now rendered so familiar that it almost ceases to excite attention. It is somewhat remarkable that, although many attempts have been made to discover it in the place of its appearance, every effort has hitherto failed of success. On approaching the spot it becomes invisible to the pursuers, even while it remains luminous to those who watch it at a distance. To trace its exact abode, a level has been taken during its appearance, by which the curious have been guided in their researches the ensuing day; but nothing has hitherto been discovered.

The scientific journal, *Nature* of 23 January, 1873, contains an account from one Howard Fox, of curious lights seen on the Lizard peninsula on 5th October, 1872. Fox was walking with a friend near RUAN MAJOR (SW 704164) when they saw "a light travelling fast over the country". The account continues:

> As there was no road in the neighbourhood we watched, and soon saw two others (lights) rising from the same place and bounding over the country till they seemed to be about thirty feet from the ground in a swampy field opposite us, when they disappeared. Another rose from the other side of the field, and after reaching the middle of the field, it also disappeared. In about ten minutes we saw five or six, but none afterwards.
>
> I have asked several farmers of the district and many of my friends if they have seen any (lights), but have only met with one

farmer who said that when a boy he used to see them on
Goonhilly Downs adjoining. The geological formation of this
district is serpentine.

To this day people report strange lights in Cornwall. One informant has
told Devereux that he has seen purple-ish lights about half a metre in
diameter dancing close to the ground in the FOUR LANES (SW 690387)
area (there is a transmission mast in this vicinity). Another tells of
similar lights that sometimes spring into appearance after rainfall not far
away in the TRESLOTHAN area (SW 650379): usually three lights
appear, about a metre from the ground, in an unmoving triangular
configuration. the lights just spring suddenly into appearance, and as
suddenly "go out". A third informant claims that lightballs are sometimes to be seen in autumn months rolling up hillsides punctuated with
the chimneys of abandoned tin mines close to PORTHTOWAN (SW
695475).

It could well be, therefore, that the legends of mystery lights relate to
unexplained natural phenomena that have been woven into the rich
tapestry of folklore.

If so, what could these lights be? An obvious answer is "Will o' the
Wisp", supposed glowing methane above bogs and cemeteries. However, it is not as well known as it ought to be that the "methane gas"
theory has never been scientifically proved. Certainly, there is no
explanation for coherent balls of light bounding around the countryside.
In any case, the lights are not necessarily always seen over swampy
areas or cemeteries. What about ball-lightning? All well and good if the
phenomenon appears during electrical storms, which is by no means
usually the case. In any event, "ball lightning" has not been explained
either – modern physics cannot at present explain how lightballs can
maintain a distinct form and move through the air.

It rather seems that there is truly exotic, and potentially important
energy produced by the Earth that currently eludes explanation.
Devereux refers to it as "earth lights" (see his *Earth Lights Revelation*,
1989). These may be related to, or be another version of, ball lightning
and earthquake lights (stressed geology is known to be able to produce
curious light effects during earthquakes) but do not require electrical
storm or earthquake conditions in order to appear. They usually haunt
localised regions – they are terrain-related. In some places, locals have
seen them for generations.

These zones have so far been found to contain recurring geological characteristics, such as significant faulting, seismic history, mineral deposits or bodies of water (which can cause micro-quakes). Detailed work in certain zones has shown an overwhelming correlation between lights incidence and surface faulting. In some zones, lights have greater incidence after a weather front has passed – this may be due to variable atmospheric pressure on the geology in the area, in addition to possible atmospheric factors.

The apparent geological connection is highlighted by many contemporary reports of strange lights seen near old mines, especially copper, tin and lead mines, and by eighteenth-century mining texts which tell of the use of lightballs emerging from the ground in the prospecting for copper veins. Recent findings regarding the Bere Alston arsenic and copper mine close to the Devon-Cornwall border near Tavistock suggest that this method of prospecting was being used up until the early years of this century! Writing in issue 114 (1991) of the Cornish-based international journal *The Ley Hunter* (Box 92, Penzance, Cornwall TR18 2BX), Ralph Ruby, a qualified engineer and retired member of the Patent Office, states: "I well remember my father telling me that when he was a boy his father would point out such (light) phenomena. My grandfather was a miner all his life working in the Bere Alston mine...My father told me that the lights occurred after certain weather conditions – usually after rain or storms – and were most noticeable towards dusk or in the evening. The lights were described as 'dancing' , 'running', 'moving', 'along (or 'near') the ground' by him...From the 'lights' my grandfather could determine the nature of the ore and the richness of the vein...I take it that this would have been perhaps 1910 or thereabouts". One particular location was near Denham Bridge, Bere Alston.

With its richly fascinating geology, it should be no surprise to find that Cornwall has its share of unusual light phenomena. And this seems to be in the minds of present day witnesses, for when he asked one of his informants what he thought caused the lights, Devereux was told: "Well, it's the radon, isn't it"?

Prime amongst current theories accounting for the light is the Tectonic Stress Theory, put forward by Professor Michael Persinger of Laurentian University in Ontario, Canada. This posits that a strain field is produced during tectonic flexing of the Earth's crust in certain areas, not necessarily leading to earthquake or tremor, and that this generalised field can move through an area, causing electrical and geomagnetic changes and focusing in certain topographical and geological configurations, producing light phenomena.

Anthropology reveals that earth lights have been seen by many cultures around the world, and are usually interpreted as spirits of one form or another – "faeries" as we have seen in Celtic lands like Cornwall, for instance. In West Africa the lights are called "aku", devil; the Penobscot Indians of Maine thought they were the spirits of shamans flying through the night or else "fire creatures" ("eskuda hit"); the Wintu of California called them "spirit eaters"; the Lapps also see the lights as flying shamans in fireball-spirit form engaged in nocturnal battles with one another; native Malaysians call them "pennangal", the spectral heads of women who have died in childbirth; Hawaiian islanders call the lights "akualele", spirits. In Brazil, globes of light are called "Mae de Ouro", Mother of Gold, as they are thought to lead to buried treasure; around Darjeeling, India, the lights are thought to be the lanterns of the Little Men, "chota admis", to go near which is to court illness or death. The Aymara Indians of the Andes have a detailed knowledge and lore concerning meteorology, and they single out curious light effects, "sullaje", which they insist are not lightning or other known meteorological phenomena.

Sullaje seems associated with mountain peaks, and light phenomena has been associated with many "holy" mountains and hills, such as Mount Taishan, China; Mount Athos, Greece; Glastonbury Tor, England; Mount Omberg, Sweden; Mount Sorte, Venezuela; Mount Shasta, USA and many more.

It is clear that the lights have been seen as manifestations of deity in some cultures, for temples have been built dedicated to them. A tower in a temple complex on a peak of Mount Taishan, for instance, was built specifically to observe the "Bodhisattva lights". A temple at Purnigiri, India, is dedicated to the lights that habitually appear around the site (the temple is built over a fault). There is even a Christian chapel dedicated to "St Mary of the Lights" in the Swiss Alps, referring to the lightballs that travellers there report from time to time, and which are seen as being helpful, if somewhat mysterious, guides in bad weather. It may be that prehistoric standing stones in western Europe were likewise raised in honour of places haunted by light phenomena, and which were perceived as being spirits or deific manifestations: a long list is developing of historical accounts and modern eyewitness reports of lights at such megalithic sites, and Cornwall is, of course, well endowed with megalithic remains.

There have been many interpretations of the lights in Western society over the centuries. The longest-lived was that they were the fiery breath of dragons: the matter was the subject of scholarly debate during the middle Ages. In Denmark and Germany, particularly, strange lights were known as "treasure lights", hovering over buried treasure. There were "faeries", "piskies", "omens", "ghostly lanterns", "spirits" too, we have seen, and in more recent times they have been seen as enemy airships and, in World War Two, "foo fighters". Now, they have been caught up in the "UFO" interpretation, though in some areas, particularly in the USA, they are sometimes still seen as ghosts or "spooklights" such as at Marfa, Texas, where strange lights out on the desert have been reported for over a century.

Typically, earth lights appear as "basketball-sized" globes, but smaller and larger ones have also been reliably reported. Also, the lights can take on many shapes other than globular, and can hover, fly rapidly, perform aerobatic manoeuvre, merge together, and so on. They have been photographed, by individual witnesses and by teams, such as the group which studied an outbreak of lights in the Hessdalen valley, Norway, in the early-mid 1980s, and the university group that studied the Piedmont lights outbreak in southern Missouri in the late 1970s.

The nature of the light energy is not known, but it seems to favour the vicinity of charge collectors like TV masts, isolated buildings on or near faulting, high tension cables and mountain peaks.

Although the nature of the light energy seems therefore to have electromagnetic aspects, there are more exotic reported characteristics as well. These include the ability of the lights to assume coherent shapes, as well as to shapeshift; the lights can sometimes be seen from one direction but not from another (as seems to have been the case with the St Austell light described above); they can sometimes exhibit rapidly alternating signs of having mass and being weightless; they can sometimes burn vegetation and witnesses, yet at other times have no effect. They may represent some kind of "macro-quantum" effect occurring in nature.

There are two even more bizarre reported characteristics of the lights. The energy fields associated with them can perhaps cause altered states of consciousness in close encounter witnesses, creating hallucinatory effects that can be very dependent on a person's expectations and culture

– thus perhaps explaining why earlier people saw "fairies" and we nowadays see "aliens". (Such energy fields may also be responsible for the occasionally-reported "poltergeist" effects in the vicinity of earth lights outbreaks. These effects include not only disembodied voices, but a crunching sound on the ground, metal doorlatches moving of their own accord, objects flying about, and even cases of metal utensils twisting and warping).

Secondly, the lights may even possess rudimentary intelligence themselves: there are a number of instances on record in which lights have seemed to interact with witnesses, responding to their voices or gestures, or hopping out of the way of flashlight beams!

Perhaps, after all, the old explanation or "spirits", "faeries" and whatnot, is not too far from the mark ...

(The authors would be pleased to hear from any readers who have witnessed "earth lights", especially in Cornwall).

7

Legends of Arthur

No single name of legend or history can fire the imagination as much as that of King Arthur. To this day, arguments rage as to whether such a king ever existed or, if he did, who he really was. Historians and the earliest traditions agree on the original scenario of the Arthurian legends; the 5th or 6th centuries AD, immediately following the with-drawal of the Roman legions from Britain, and when the settlement of Anglo-Saxons from Germany and the Low Countries – the ancestors of the English – on Britain's east coast were posing a serious threat to the Celtic population. Despite those later traditions which declare Arthur "King of England", he is remembered as a great leader of the Celtic resistance against the Germanic newcomers.

Perhaps the best identification of this shadowy king equates him with a High King of the Britons who reigned from 464 to 470 AD. Recorded only by a title of respect, "Riotamus" (British "rigo-tamos" – high or supreme king), he died in Gaul, fighting alongside the Gallo-Roman forces against the invading Goths, and after having been betrayed.

Even early Welsh traditions indicate that Arthur was strongly associa-ted with south-western Britain and it is noticeable that the firmest of them are located in Somerset and Cornwall, both of which were part of the post-Roman kingdom of Dumnonia.

Of all the hundreds of Arthurian locations in Britain, only one claims to have been his birth-place: TINTAGEL (SX 050890). Unfortunately, modern tourism has tended to swamp Tintagel with spurious claims which have nothing to do with tradition: that it was "Camelot", home of the Round Table and so on. Even the oft-used title "King Arthur's Castle" is not supported by tradition which, as used by Geoffrey of Monmouth in the 12th century, only claims the site to have been where Arthur was conceived. In fact, of the hundreds of locations connected with Arthur, only Tintagel is cited as his birthplace. Even the earliest folk tales populate Tintagel Castle with other kings, most notably King Mark.

Of the hundreds of locations associated with Arthur, only Tintagel is cited as his birthplace (C. Weatherhill)

For sixty years, following excavations in the 1920s, it has been believed that the great headland held a Celtic monastery of the 5th and 6th centuries, but more modern research and excavation has now provided a far more exciting picture of early Tintagel.

From the 5th or the 7th centuries AD, Tintagel was indeed a stronghold and the huge quantities of Mediterranean pottery found there show it to have been a major tribute centre; in other words, a place of great importance. The generally agreed opinion of Tintagel is now that it was a seat, probably a seasonal or ceremonial one, of the kings of Dumnonia.

It has therefore become a much more feasible location for the birthplace
of Arthur than the theoretic monastery could have been.

*It is now generally agreed that, between the 5th and 7th centuries AD, Tintagel was not
a monastery but a seasonal or ceremonial seat of the Kings of Dumnonia (C. Weatherhill)*

Strangely, though, the professional archaeologists veer away from the
subject of Arthur as if it contains some sort of stigma to their credibility.
They categorically state that Tintagel had no connection whatsoever with
Arthur, but without providing reasons for their denial. In my view, this
attitude does them no credit at all. It may be that legend has grown so
huge that it has become forbidden territory to their circle but, in my
view, such flat denial and apparent refusal to seriously research the

subject does their profession little credit, especially when they accept as real other characters of early history for whom there is even less actual evidence than there is for Arthur.

An often cited opinion is that Geoffrey of Monmouth himself was responsible for the tradition of Tintagel as the birthplace of Arthur, but Geoffrey was a stranger to Cornwall. Why should he have chosen such a location? All that existed on the headland in his time were the confused remains of early buildings, and a huge ditch on the approach to its narrow neck. the castle whose remains perch on the dark crags today did not exist in Geoffrey's time; it was built in the early 13th century by Richard, Earl of Cornwall. It seems more likely that he actually heard such a tradition and included it into his fanciful tale which, as Geoffrey Ashe has brilliantly demonstrated in his book *The Discovery of King Arthur* actually consists of twists and embellishments of verifiable facts.

On a flat rock surface situated on the southern side of the headland's flat top is King Arthur's footprint, an artificial cavity in the life sized shape of a left foot. One theory is that this featured in coronation ceremonies, with the newly crowned monarch's foot firmly inserted in the footprint to symbolise his rule over the land.

Geoffrey's story was that King Uther Pendragon lusted after Igraine, wife of Gorlois, Duke of Cornwall (King of Dumnonia?). Gorlois shut her in the impregnable fortress of Tintagel while he engaged Uther's troops in battle at his fort of Dameliock. This was conjectured to have been TREGEARE ROUNDS (SX 033800) near Pendoggett, but without any real foundation. In fact the name, which was recorded in the Domesday Book as Demelihoc, still exists today as Domellick. This is at the eastern foot of a conical hill on which stands the church of ST DENNIS (SW 951583), not named after any saint but after the Cornish word "dinas", a fort. Its circular churchyard preserves the shape of an ancient hill fort, almost certainly the original Dameliock.

Gorlois is an actual Cornish personal name, occurring in place-names as Gorlas, and probably meaning "grey man" or, intriguingly, "green man". At Dameliock he died, whilst Uther, transformed into the likeness of Gorlois by the arts of Merlin, gained unchallenged entry to Tintagel, and into Igraine's bed. The result was Arthur.

The headland of Tintagel is pierced through by Merlin's Cave which, as it is filled at high water, must have provided the old magician with an uncomfortably wet existence. It must be said, however, that the cavern's link with Merlin is only as recent as the Victorian romanticists.

*Castle-an-dinas, near St Columb, served as the young Arthur's hunting lodge
(C. Weatherhill)*

Although Arthur is found in legends and traditions from Cornwall to
southern Scotland, the strongest links seem to indicate that he was a
Dumnonian. Legend says that he grew up in Cornwall, where CASTLE-
AN-DINAS (SW 946624), the hill fort near St Columb Major, served as
his hunting lodge while he hunted the marshy wilds of GOSS MOOR to
the south. On one occasion his horse left a hoofprint in a rock, and this is
the recently rediscovered capstone of a destroyed dolmen called the
DEVIL'S COYT (SW 923619).

Early Welsh tradition actually allots a Cornish fortress to Arthur.
Named as Kelliwic or Celli Wig, this might have been CASTLE KILLI-
BURY (KELLY ROUNDS) (SX 019736) near Wadebridge or, even more
likely, CASTLE CANYKE (SX 086658) at Bodmin which commanded an

important trans-peninsular route and which has the place-name Callywith only a mile away. The town of CALLINGTON (SX 360697), once Caellwic, has been ruled out on the grounds that this old name is Anglo-Saxon and therefore much later than Arthur.

King Arthur's Hall, a curious and unexplained enclosure in lonely isolation on the expanse of Bodmin Moor (C. Weatherhill)

The expanses of Bodmin Moor contain further places associated with Arthur, although no tales are preserved. KING ARTHUR'S HALL (SX 130777) is a curious rectangular embanked enclosure, its sides internally revetted by 56 upright stones up to 1.8 metres in height. The flat interior is damp and boggy and the entire structure has not significantly altered since it was described, apparently for the first time, in 1584. The Hall's function is a mystery, as is its age. It might be as old as the Neolithic period, or as recent as the medieval. Close by, on KING ARTHUR'S DOWNS (SX 135775), are a pair of stone circles.

On the eastern side of Bodmin Moor, KING ARTHUR'S BED (SX 240757), is a roughly man-shaped natural rock basin on Trewartha Tor, and the great dolmen of TRETHEVY QUOIT (SX 259688), near St Cleer, has been called Arthur's Quoit.

King Arthur's Bed, a man-shaped rock basin on Trewortha Tor (C. Weatherhill)

St Nectan's Kieve, where the Grail Knights bowed their heads in prayer before the perilous quest (C. Weatherhill)

Closer to Tintagel, the secluded, magical glen and spectacular waterfall at ST NECTAN'S KIEVE (SX 080885 – See Chapter 3) is said to have been where the Grail Knights bowed their heads in prayer before setting out on their perilous quest. The Quest for the Grail represents a pagan myth, also found in other European cultures, of the descent into the Underworld by a hero in order to restore fertility and life to a barren winter world.

The Land's End peninsula has an Arthurian mythos all its own. When Robert Hunt sought out local legends in the 19th century, he was told by an old man at PENDEEN (SW 382343) that the land thereabouts once teemed with giants until Arthur came to vanquish them. The great Iron Age cliff castle of TRERYN DINAS (SW 398222), on Penwith's south coast, is claimed to have been in Arthur's possession (some recent books have mistaken this for a similarly named cliff castle on the north coast at Gurnard's Head).

One of the most powerful tales of Arthur in this region is that of the Battle of Vellan-druchar; a tradition which has inexplicably been omitted from a number of recent publications about Arthur. This tells of a landing of the "Sea Kings" or "Danes" at GWENVER (SW 363277), near Sennen Cove, following several unopposed raids. This time, they landed in large numbers, set on penetrating deep inland. They crossed the peninsula to the north coast, destroying as they went, but the chain of warning beacons had already been lit, sending the alarm quickly through the length of Cornwall.

As the invading army made their way back to their ships, they were met by Arthur who, with nine kings, had marched down from eight Tintagel or Kelliwic. The battle was fought at VELLAN-DRUCHAR (SW 423263), a mile 'east of St Buryan, and was so fierce that the nearby millwheel was worked with blood. Some accounts claim that this was Kemyel Mill, two miles away, but this is in error. Kemyel Mill was worked by a different stream.

The battle was a crushing victory by Arthur, whose men pursued the surviving invaders westward to their ships at Gwenver, but during their absence a local wise-woman had raised a westerly gale by emptying the holy well against the hill, and sweeping the church, possibly the destroyed Chapel Idne at Sennen Cove, from door to altar. The gale and tide had driven the ships up the beach, stranding them. The remaining invaders were killed, and the ships rotted where they lay.

Arthur and the nine kings pledged themselves in the holy well and the victory feast was held on the TABLE-MAEN (SW 359258). Such large, flat-topped rocks were once a common feature in settlements near Land's End. Each known as the Carack Zans (Sacred Rock), the Table-Maen is the only one to survive. It was at this feast that Merlin appeared to utter one of his typically gloomy prophecies, as detailed later on.

The legend of the victory feast attaches itself to at least two other stones: at BOSAVERN (SW 371303) near St Just, and the FOUR PARISHES STONE (SW 430354). The latter may actually have been associated with another legendary battle, that of Goon-adga-idniall, where the Rialobran named on the nearby Men Scryfa (Stone of Writing) was slain. Some modern books have wrongly added the dolmen of Lanyon Quoit to this list.

William Hals, writing c.1700 and since quoted by others, claimed that it was seven Saxon kings who dined on the Table-Maen at about the year 600. He destroyed his own argument by naming them: Cissa of the South Saxons lived about a century before the time and, while the rest did flourish in the late 6th and early 7th centuries, Aethelberht of Kent was actually dead 16 years before his alleged fellow-diner Penda of Mercia came to power. Historically, the Saxon advance on Dumnonia was still some way east of Exeter at this time, and for Saxon kings from as far afield as Northumbria, Mercia and Kent to have travelled un-scathed to the Land's End would have been a total impossibility.

Arthur's nine kings are intriguing. They may represent the typically Celtic "three times three" exaggeration and therefore only have been three kings or, more likely, three commanders. This would suggest three war-hosts of a hundred men each which had marched from north-east Cornwall; the old region of Trigg, or "Pagus Tricurius" – the land of the three war-hosts.

The Vellan-druchar story takes place at a time centuries too early for the Danes to have been involved. If, for "Danes", one reads "Saxons", the scenario for such a battle becomes historically feasible. In the 5th century, there was a Saxon pirate base on the river Loire in western France and it is known that they made a thorough nuisance of them-selves not only on Biscay coasts but also in the Celtic Sea, where they launched two major raids on Ireland, the second in the year 471. It would have been logical for them to have stopped for shelter and provisions at a halfway point – the Land's End peninsula of Cornwall.

Some historians believe that Vellan-druchar was actually a campaign of Aethelstan c.930, and that Arthur's name has been substituted for his.

There are certainly tales that Aethelstan fought a battle in Penwith but, in fact there is no actual evidence that he ever set foot in Cornwall. Even his alleged granting of a charter to St Buryan church (itself rather suspect) could easily have been done from Exeter without him having to actually visit the place.

BOSIGRAN CASTLE (SW 417370), another Iron Age cliff castle, has been linked to the Arthurian legend due to interpretation of its name as "dwelling of Igraine", the name of Arthur's mother. Unfortunately, early spellings of this name show that it actually means "dwelling by the home of a crane (bird)".

In the "Mabinogion", the tale of Culhwch and Olwen details the hunt for the boar Twrch Trwyth by Arthur's men. At one point, the hunted boar runs through Cornwall to the headland of "Penrhyn Awstin" before taking to the sea. The name is not known in Cornwall, but could it have been "Penryn an stean" – promontory of tin, and therefore Penwith?

On Slaughter Bridge itself, Arthur is said to have slain the traitor Mordred before succumbing to his own wounds (C. Weatherhill)

It was Geoffrey of Monmouth who first located Arthur's fateful last battle, Camlann, in Cornwall. He called it Camblan, thereby combining the two names of The River Camel, formerly called the Alan. SLAUGHTER BRIDGE (SX 109857), near Camelford, is cited as the location of the battle and, on the bridge itself, Arthur is said to have slain the traitor Mordred before succumbing to his own wounds. A large inscribed stone beside the stream close by was said to have marked the King's tomb. The final letters of the inscription LATINI IC IACIT FILIVS MAGARI, were once misread as ATRY and seen as a contraction of the name Arthur.

The traditions of the King's sword having been thrown into a Cornish lake are comparatively recent. DOZMARY POOL (SX 194746) is the nearest lake to Slaughter Bridge, even though 8 miles separates them, and its Otherworldly atmospheres and traditions lent themselves well to the role of Excalibur's resting place. Tennyson, when composing his epic "Idylls of the King", chose LOE POOL (SW 645242) for the sword's resting place.

In Cornish tradition, the spirit of Arthur lives on in the form of either a raven or a chough, whose legs and beak are red, thereby recalling the bloodiness of the King's last battle. In the 19th century, an old man at Marazion rebuked a man who had shot at a raven, saying that Arthur was alive in the form of such a bird.

Through the legend of the lost land of Lyonesse, recounted in Chapter 11, the Isles of Scilly are strongly associated with the King. Three of the Eastern Isles are named Great, Middle and Little Arthur. They bear a number of megalithic tombs, the largest of which, on the crest of GREAT ARTHUR (SW 942135), has been put forward as a possible resting place of the King himself.

MERLIN, Arthur's magician, adviser and prophet, also has Cornish associations. His name, originally Myrddin (pronounced Merthen), was changed by Geoffrey of Monmouth who considered its Latinised form, Merdinus, to be too close to a French vulgarity for comfort. Interestingly, the name Merthen Point occurs within a mile of Penwith's Arthurian fort of Treryn Dinas where Merlin predicted that when the key of the castle (a natural formation – see Chapter 1) was removed, the Logan Rock (the great rocking stone on the headland) would topple and the castle sink back beneath the sea. When, in 1824, Lieutenant Hugh Goldsmith's sailors forced the Key out of its hole in the rocks, and prised the Logan off its perch, two parts of the prophecy were fulfilled. The castle, though, stubbornly remained above the waves.

In Cornwall, Merlin is remembered for his melancholy predictions, one of which was at the victory feast of the Table-Maen after the Battle of Vellan-druchar. Here, in Hunt's wonderful phrase, he was "seized by the prophetic afflatus" and intoned that:

"The Northmen wild once more will land; And bleach their bones on Escalls' sand; The soil of Vellan-druchar's plain; Again will take a sanguine stain; And o'er the millwheel roll a flood; Of Danish mixed with Cornish blood; When thus the vanquished find no tomb; Expect the dreadful day of doom". He also proclaimed that a similar feast at the Table-maen would be a prelude to the end of the world.

At an infant MOUSEHOLE (SW 470263), he was no less comforting, and here his prophecy was recorded in Cornish:

"E ra teera warn mean Merlin; Ra leske Pawle, Penzans ha Newlen" (He shall land on the stone of Merlin; Who shall burn Paul, Penzance and Newlyn).

In 1595, four Spanish warships appeared out of the Mount's Bay mists and a massive shore party put Mousehole, Paul, Newlyn and Penzance to the torch before setting back to their French base. The settlements were burned to the ground and only one building in Mousehole survived (the Keigwin Manor house, which can still be seen). The original Merlin Rock was situated where Mousehole harbour's southern quay now stands; the name has been transferred to a sea-washed ledge to the south.

Merlin vies with St Selevan in being the prophet who said of the split stone in ST LEVAN churchyard (SW 380222):

"When with panniers astride; A packhorse can ride;
Through St Levan's Stone; The world will be done".

Also in West Cornwall, Merlin stated of the once sensitive loggan (rocking) stone called MEN AMBER (SW 651323), on a hill above Nancegollan, that it would stand " Till England had no king". During the Civil War, Shrubsall's Roundheads deliberately dislodged the stone, ruining its poise. Merlin seems to have been doubly prophetic here: in his time, the coining of the term "England" still lay several centuries in the future.

He also said of two south coast headlands: "When Rame Head and the Dodman meet; Man and Woman will have cause to greet (i.e. weep)". These promontories remain 25 miles apart; however, during the

Wars of the Roses, Rame Head, formerly the property of the Edgecumbe family, came into the possession of the Bodrugans who owned the Dodman. In this way, it could be argued that the two headlands "met".

Blight's drawing of Men Amber, which stood 'til England had no king

Finally, as will be detailed in Chapter 11, it was Merlin's ghost that cast the dreadful spell which drowned the land of Lyonesse beneath the Atlantic after the Battle of Camlann, so destroying the traitorous Mordred.

Through the "Mabinogion", and the early bardic poem "Lament for Gerent", GERENT of Cornwall has become firmly linked to the Arthurian legend. It would appear that Cornwall, or more correctly, Dumnonia, had two kings of this name. The second lived at around the year 700 and was the recipient of a letter from the Synod of Whitby insisting that the Celtic church in his kingdom conform to the doctrines of Rome. The first Gerent lived about a century earlier, though a good hundred years after any historical Arthur, and was, according to early genealogies, the father of St Just, St Levan (Yestin and Selyf), and his successor, Cado. he may also have been the "Gereint rac deheu" (Gerent for the South) who fought in a fierce battle at Catraeth (Catterick, Yorkshire) in 598.

Gerent is closely associated with the Roseland peninsula of South Cornwall, where the village of GERRANS (SW 873352) recalls his name. Traditionally, his castle lay to the north of Gerrans and is now called DINGEREIN CASTLE (SW 882375). When Gerent died, his body was rowed across the bay in a golden boat with silver oars to be buried, along with the fabulous ship, beneath the huge barrow of CARNE BEACON (SW 913387) to the south of Veryan. This huge mound was excavated in 1855, but no trace of the golden ship was found. However, it has to be said that the dig concentrated on the centre, where a large stone cist was found, and that most of the barrow remains undisturbed. An interesting link with this legend is found in the older name for Dingerin Castle which was formerly Cargurrel, "fort of the ship". A further legend relates that a tunnel called Mermaid's Hole connects Dingerein to the sea.

One of the most famous Arthurian stories, that of TRISTAN, ISOLDE and KING MARK, not only has a Cornish setting, but has been recently shown to have been of Cornish origin before its publication as a romance by the 12th century French poet Beroul.

Tristan, born in Lyonesse – probably Leonois, Brittany, rather than Cornwall's drowned land – came to the court of his uncle King Mark of Cornwall at TINTAGEL. In Beroul's poem, Mark also reigned from Lancien, now LANTYAN (SX 105573) near the banks of the Fowey estuary, only a mile and a half north of CASTLE DORE (SX 103548), an Iron Age fort often linked with Mark. As Mark's champion, Tristan slew the Irish champion Morholt on the unlocated St Sampson's Isle. Poisoned by a wound inflicted by Morholt, Tristan travelled to Ireland for healing, concealing his real identity. There he met Isolde the Fair, daughter of King Anguish (Aengus?) and later brought her back to Cornwall to be Mark's bride.

During the journey, the pair were accidentally given a love potion by Branwen, Isolde's handmaiden, which had been intended for Mark. Tristan and the Irish beauty fell in love but the arranged marriage had to go ahead. In order to disguise the fact that Isolde had lost her virginity to Tristan, the "bride" in Mark's bed on the wedding night was, in fact, Branwen.

Through the spying of the dwarf Frocin, Mark grew suspicious of Tristan and eventually the lovers were caught. Tristan escaped his captors by leaping from the window of the clifftop chapel variously located at CHAPEL POINT (SX 028433) near Mevagissey, and at ST CATHERINE'S POINT (SX 119509), Fowey.

St Catherine's Point, Fowey – perhaps the site of Tristan's leap (C. Weatherhill)

Together, Tristan and Isolde fled to the Forest of Morrois, now recalled by the place-name MORESK (SW 849433) near Truro. On the way, they visited the hermit Ogrin, whose hermitage has, without any real foundation, been put forward as the chapel on the weird ROCHE ROCK (SX 991596). They were discovered and spared by Mark, and Isolde returned to the king, making an offering of her silken robe to the church of St Sampson at GOLANT (SX 121552).

Later, after being carried ashore on the back of a disguised Tristan at a river crossing at MALPAS (SW 845428), Isolde is able to swear to Mark that no man had come between her thighs except he who had carried her ashore. This assertion takes place at Mark's hunting lodge in Blancheland, probably near Kea, an area once called "Alba Landa" and the present place-names CHYWYNE and CHIRWIN (SW 805412) may derive from the medieval Cornish "tyr gwyn" – white land. Not far away, the Iron Age fort of GOODERN (SW 789431) is associated with both Mark and the King Teudar who persecuted the Irish saints.

At last accepting that he will never gain the woman he loves, Tristan returns to Brittany, where he marries another Isolde, called "Of the White Hands", but is unable to consummate the marriage. Mortally wounded in battle, he sends for the healing arts of Isolde the Fair, but his jealous wife lies to him, saying that the approaching ship has black sails, meaning that Isolde the Fair is not on board. This news causes Tristan to give up his fight for life and when Isolde the Fair lands to find that Tristan has died, she dies of grief. Mark causes both bodies to be returned to Cornwall where they are buried together.

On the approaches to Fowey stands the TRISTAN STONE (SX 110524), the original site of which was at the Four Turnings nearby. 2.7 metres tall, this majestic stone bears the inscription DRUSTANS HIC IACIT CVNOMORI FILIVS: Drustans (the original name from which Tristan is derived) lies here, son of Cunomorus ("sea-hound"). This second name became Cynvawr, and a king of Dumnonia in the early 6th century bore this very name. In the 9th century, in his "Life of St Paul Aurelian", the Breton monk Wrmonoc wrote of the king "Marcus, whom men call by another name, Quonomorius". Was Tristan the son of Mark, and not his nephew?

In the 16th century, antiquary John Leland saw another line of inscription on the stone which said, CUM DOMINA OUSILLA: with the lady Ousilla. This name is an acceptable Latin form of the British name ADSILTIA, "she who should be gazed on", which in Cornish became Eselt. This name, in turn, was grotesquely altered by continental writers to Iseult/Isoude/Isolde. A 10th century record of a place name includes this name: "Hryt Eseld" – Eselt's ford – on a stream in the Lizard peninsula near PORTHALLOW (SW 797232) and, coincidentally, not far from another fortification connected with King Teudar at LESTOWDER (SW 793247). This third line of the Tristan Stone has gone and comparisons of the stone with drawings by Dr Borlase in the 18th century would indicate that one side of it might have broken away.

Could it be possible that this majestic 6th century memorial actually contained the names of all three of the main characters in the world's most famous love tragedy?

The majestic Tristan Stone – does this commemorate the tragic hero? (C. Weatherhill)

8

Witchcraft

It is perhaps unfortunate that the popular picture of a witch almost universally portrays a black clad old harridan, with pointed hat, nutcracker jaw and warts, cackling her incantations over a seething cauldron, summoning the legions of evil to wreak havoc upon the world. With black cat and broomstick, such a creature recalls the embodiment of wickedness and has done ever since Shakespeare wrote Macbeth.

The popular view is only a small part of witchcraft. Although Cornwall, and Britain as a whole, had its share of black witches, the vast majority of witches – a term which covers both men and women – worked mainly for the good of their communities through, for example healing by the arts of herblore. Even so, religious zealots have, through the centuries, hounded such people. Thousands have died horribly for little more reason than ignorance and prejudice; many for the "crimes" of being old, living alone, taken to muttering to themselves, owning a cat and professing knowledge of herbal healing.

In Cornwall, a deep-rooted belief in the powers of witchcraft lasted rather longer than in many other places due to its relative isolation from the centres of "civilisation". The arts of magic are very much survivals of pre-Christian practices and, indeed, there are quite a number of people in the Duchy today who subscribe to the pagan religions and practice as witches. Such people may not be necessarily obvious; the quiet, well-mannered man or woman in the office or behind the bank counter might well be a modern witch.

It has to be remembered that the Cornish, like other Celts, are naturally people of the country and the sea, whose lives have been ruled by the natural elements they worshipped before Christianity – and often since. It therefore followed that such elements of raw power could be brought to obey the will of those who possessed the powers of the occult.

There have been hundreds of Cornish witches, the far western Penwith peninsula containing the greatest number. Here, the parishes of

Zennor and St Levan were particularly noted for their witches, with St Buryan not far behind. The "Zennor Charmers", with the power to charm away sickness, wounds and "ill-wishing", were such sought after, and the inhabitants of St Levan went under the collective name of "St Levan Witches", such was their reputation.

Those who were reputed to be "black witches" were usually accused of employing the practice of "ill-wishing" or "overlooking"; casting even spells on people's health or livelihoods. Even today, it is not unusual to hear of a pale or sickly looking person being described as "wisht", a contraction of "ill-wished". Sometimes, these black witches possessed the power of shape-shifting into the form of an animal – toads and white hares were particularly popular choices.

A woman who lived at TREWEY (SW 454383) near Zennor was reputed to possess such powers, but these were ridiculed by her boorish husband who, on returning home one evening to find no dinner on the table, gave her a tongue-lashing. But, no money, no food and as she said: "Harsh words butter no parsnips". His reply was to sneeringly invite her to use her supposed powers and added that if there was no meal for him within half an hour, it would be the worse for her. She immediately set off for St Ives, five miles away, and the husband, to his everlasting horror, saw her change shape into that of a hare which sped off into the distance. She walked back in through the door, laden with food, within the half-hour and, from that day, her husband went in fear and loathing of her. When the Witch of Trewey died, a black cloud hovered over the house. As her coffin was borne off to the church, a hare leapt over the coffin, causing the bearers to drop it in their fright. More men picked up the coffin, on which a cat materialised and again it was abandoned. Further bearers were persuaded to carry it the remaining distance to the churchyard and the service began. As the clergyman uttered the words: "I am the resurrection and the life", the hare again appeared, uttered a chilling howl, changed into a black, misshapen creature and vanished.

One way of removing a spell of ill-wishing was for the victim to draw blood from the witch and numerous cases of this have been recorded, including some which became 19th century court cases. In an earlier case, heard at PENZANCE (SW 474303) in 1686, Betty Seeze and Jane Noel stood accused of having bewitched John Tonkin, causing him to vomit walnut shells, straws, nails and a netmaker's needle.

Sometimes a sacrifice was required to remove the spell. For example, a farmer near PORTREATH (SW 656453) burned alive a calf in order to remove a spell which had caused disease in his cattle and horses. In 1890, a hare was walled up in a newly-built house at FALMOUTH (SW 810320). The builder gave the reason that, since ground had been taken, something must be given back to the "outside gods".

On the island of ST MARTIN'S in the Isles of Scilly (SV 930155), a woman whose sheep fell mysteriously sick was advised by a male Penzance witch that they been bewitched and that the malevolent spirit responsible dwelt within the body of an old mare kept in the same field. Consequently the wretched animal was burnt to death.

To become a witch seems to have been quite easy. To touch one of Cornwall's numerous loggan, or rocking, stones nine times at midnight, was all that was required in order to gain such powers. An alternative method was to climb onto Zennor's GIANT'S ROCK (SW 454387) without moving it. Although solidly set today, it was at one time a sensitive loggan and, if the task was performed successfully, the powers granted were, presumably, considerable.

Just to the east of Zennor, the hillside near Eagle's Nest was formerly known as BURN DOWNS (SW 465385). here, on the eve of Midsummer, all the witches of the west gathered to celebrate the solstice, burning their great fires on each carn, dolmen and rock basin. A huge square boulder was the Witches' Rock. According to one source, this was broken up by stonemasons in the 19th century, probably at the instigation of Wesleyan fervour. Its loss is a sad one, for to touch it nine times – again, the magical three times three – a midnight would insure against bad luck.

One of West Cornwall's most notorious black witches was Madge Figgy of RAFTRA (SW 376233) who was not only the leader of the fearsome St Levan witches, but also of the local wrecking crew. Modern tourism loves to tell of the Cornish wreckers who lured ships onto the rocks by shining false lights. This is modern invention. No such case occurs anywhere in recorded history and only once in legend – and even then the responsible party was a stranger to Cornwall. Madge Figgy, though, had her own way of encouraging shipwrecks to happen. She would sit in a giant natural chair on the great cliff pinnacle of the Chair Ladder at TOL-PEDN-PENWITH (SW 365216) and cast spells to summon storms.

The Chair Ladder, Madge Figgy's accustomed perch (P. Devereux)

Many wrecks, the victims of Madge Figgy's storms, were washed into Por Loe, to be plundered (P. Devereux)

Madge Figgy has no mention prior to Robert Hunt's 1881 collection of legends. She seems to have succeeded an earlier witch, a man, known as Harry the Hermit of CHAPEL CARN BREA (SW 386281). He appears in a story by Newlyn writer Nicholas Boson, which was written between 1660 and 1700, called "The Duchess of Cornwall's Progress", possibly based on a real visit to the area by Catherine of Braganza. In this, Harry the Hermit, dwelling "in his state and gravity" in the tiny chapel which formerly stood on the great Neolithic cairn on the hilltop, was accused of witchcraft by the Dean of St Buryan; charges which Boson rendered in the Cornish of his time:

"Rag an Arlothas an wolas Kernow.

Dreth gwz Kibmias Benigas, Why ra Cavas dreeu an gwas Harry ma Poddrack broas.

Kensa: Urt an hagar auall iggeva gweel ldo derevoll warneny keniffer termen drerany moas durt pedden an wolas do sillan &c.

Nessa: urt an skavoll Crackan codna iggeva setha war en crees an aules ewhall heb drogi veeth.

Tregya: urt an Gurroll iggeva gweell gen askern skooth davas &c".

Literally, this means:

"*for the Lady of the Land of Cornwall.*
By your Blessed Leave, You will find that this fellow Harry is a great Witch.
First: by the storms he does make to arise on us every time that we go from the Land's End to Scilly &c.
Second: by the Break-neck chair he does sit upon the high cliff without any harm.
Third: by the boat he does fashion from a sheep's shoulder bone &c".

Boson's own extended translation makes it clear that the "break-neck chair", is at Tol-Pedn-Penwith; the chair of "Harry an Lader" (Harry the Thief), which probably explains its present name of the Chair Ladder. The boat he conjured from a sheep's shoulder blade he sailed from the great cavern at the foot of Tol-Pedn's great funnel hole. To put a stop to this, local folk took to boring a hole through such bones before disposing of them.

The great cairn and former chapel of Chapel Carn Brea, where dwelt Harry the Hermit
'in his state and gravity'

The practices of Madge Figgy and Harry the Hermit recall the tales of witches "calling down the wind" and, one time, witches used to gather at BOSCASTLE HARBOUR (SX 095915) at sailing times, to "sell the wind". For their money, the sailors received a string with three knots.

Undoing the first would bring a breeze to sail by, the second would keep a gale behind the ship, and the third was best for the wind that would guide them into harbour.

The funnel cave at Tol-pedn-penwith, from where Harry the Hermit sailed his magical craft (C. Weatherhill)

Madge Figgy and her fellow witches often congregated at Tol-Pedn, or at the Castle Peak, a tall pinnacle at TRERYN DINAS (SW 398220), from where they would take to the air to wreak their own havoc as far afield as Wales or Spain. Few local witches used the traditional broomstick; they favoured ragwort stems.

A further story of Madge Figgy is told by Hunt, although Bottrell's older version gives the witch in question as one Betty Trenoweth of ST BURYAN (SW 410258). She was on the verge of buying a pig at market when a neighbour and possible relative, Tom Trenoweth, outbid her. The witch made sure that, no matter how much the pig ate, it would steadily get thinner. After some time, and the pig getting even leaner, Tom began to despair. He decided to sell the animal and set out to drive it to Penzance market. The pig had other ideas, and bolted, leading Tom a merry chase over hill, bog and stream before he caught it. Binding its lead rope firmly to his wrist, Tom set off again. This time a hare – almost certainly the witch in that shape – leapt out in front of them, causing the pig to run off in panic, dragging Tom behind it, until it became stuck fast in the bolt under the road in Tregonebris Bottoms. Try as he might, Tom could not get the pig out until sunset, when the witch appeared on the scene. She offered Tom a twopenny loaf and half the original price of the pig and eventually Tom gave in and agreed. The witch nonchalantly approached the bolt, whispered "Chee-ah"! and the pig came out and followed her home like a dog.

Other black witches of West Cornwall included Old Joan of ALSIA MILL (SW 395252 – pron. 'aylia') who specialised in ill-wishing; and Bet of the Mill from LAMORNA (SW 447247).

At the other end of Cornwall, at ANTONY (SX 400547), lived Aunt Alsey, a reputed witch. Her landlord and his wife, who lived in Devonport, were discussing Alsey's rent arrears. They had been to Antony to threaten the old woman with eviction, but all they got was a stream of curses on the landlord's wife and the child she was carrying. In the middle of the discussion, a huge toad fell from the rafters. The landlord caught it up with tongs and hurled it into the fire. It survived, although badly burnt, and when seen trying to climb out, the landlord again took up the tongs with a view to pitching the creature out of doors. At that moment, the message was brought that Aunt Alsey had fallen into her own fire. When she died of her injuries, the toad also perished, having been sent by the witch to carry her curses to the landlord's home.

One of Cornwall's most powerful magicians has a much more European flavour to him; the Lord of Pengersick. As the young and handsome heir to PENGERSICK CASTLE (SW 582283), near Praa Sands (pron. 'pray'), he fell under the acquisitive eye of an older woman belonging to the Godolphin family. When he resisted her advances, she turned to the Witch of FRADDAM (SW 590347) for love potions and philtres. These backfired and, in desperation, she married the young Pengersick's father, a widower and, in spite, began to poison the old man's mind against his son, to the point where he paid Moorish pirates to kidnap the youth and sell him into slavery.

The young Pengersick escaped these plots and was forced to flee to the lands of the Saracens where, hearing of great magicians in a mountain fastness, he journeyed to receive their instruction. As a result, he became an accomplished sorcerer. Armed with these gifts, he returned home on hearing of the death of his father, bringing with him his high-born Arab wife and magnificent horses. One of these was a jet-black mare that would allow only the magician, the new Lord of Pengersick, to handle and ride her; it was rumoured that the beast was his familiar, a demon in the shape of a horse. On his return, he found his stepmother shut up in a chamber of the castle, a monstrous form covered in serpent-like scales from inhaling her own poisons. When she realised that the man she believed dead had returned, she cast herself into the sea.

Pengersick extended the castle, building a new tower for his wife, and using the existing one for his own magic and alchemy. On occasions, the demons he conjured were too much even for him, but these were invariably charmed into submission by the Lady's magical music. The magician perfected an elixir, by which both he and his Lady lived for many normal life-spans. However, she could not bear the experience of outliving her children and grandchildren, stopped taking the elixir and died.

The Witch of Fraddam tried her best to destroy the enchanter by tempting his famous horse to drink a poisoned potion which would induce her to throw her lordly rider. Unfortunately for her, the witch was ignorant of the mare's demonic origins, and it was she who became confined by magic in a coffin-shaped tub. In this she sails the seas until such time as the magician sees fit to release her, and woe to the mariner who sees her.

At a late point in his story, the Lord of Pengersick was introduced into

Penwith's great saga of the giants, the story of Long Tom and Jack of the Hammer. using his magic to learn the secrets of Tom's riches, and to abduct his daughter, the enchanter is defeated by the knowledge and cunning of Jack. He is stripped of his magical trappings and the fearsome mare is reduced to demon form and finally to that of a black adder.

Shortly after this, a bronzed and silent stranger appeared in Marazion, and was often seen staring down at Pengersick Castle. Then, one night, a glow appeared in the sky. The castle was ablaze. So fierce was the fire that the castle was utterly consumed. The body of the Lord of Pengersick was never found, and the mysterious stranger was never seen again. Some said that this was the Lord's satanic master, come to claim his own. A second, 16th century, castle now stands on the site.

The origin of this story may have been the result of an altercation between a 14th century Lord of Pengersick – Henry le Fort de Pengerseke – who refused to pay tithes to Hayles Abbey, Gloucestershire, which held Germoe parish in which Pengersick stands, and assaulted the local priests and Hayles monks. For this he received the Greater Excommunication. He was reinstated some years later, but one can imagine the stories woven by the churchmen about the wicked Pengersick dynasty in the interim.

As mentioned earlier, the great majority of witches in Cornwall were of the white variety. In general, these fell into a threefold hierarchy. The lowest order were the Charmers, whose activities were usually confined to the arts of healing. A typical Charmer was Old Ann of DELABOLE (SX 070840). A local woman in agony with shingles, "wildfires", sent to aunt to take one of her handkerchiefs to Old Ann. Ann charmed the handkerchief by laying a hand upon it and chanting an incantation. When the aunt returned to the stricken woman, she found that the spell had already worked and that her niece was fully cured. The Zennor Charmers were said to be so powerful that by concentration of thought they could prevent a stuck pig from bleeding to death. Above the Charmer was the Wise Man (often "Cunning Man") or Wise-woman, to whom went people who believed that they were under an evil spell. Often the Wise Man or Woman could identify the ill-wisher but generally lacked the knowledge to break the spell. Nevertheless, they could protect people against black witchcraft as well as possessing the arts of the Charmers.

The third and most powerful class were the Conjurers or Pellars, a word which is probably a contraction of 'expeller'. The original Pellars were descendants of a fisherman from CURY (SW 678213), a man called Lutey. In some versions of his tale, he is made out to be an old man, but older ones show him to have been comparatively young. Lutey was given his powers by a grateful mermaid at POLDHU COVE (SW 665200) after he had saved her from becoming stranded by the tide. The three wishes he was granted were that he might have the power to break evil spells; to charm away illness and to have the ability to find and restore stolen goods. The mermaid's comb, by which he could call her by stroking the water, was said to have remained in the family for generations.

A notable Pellar actually lived across the Tamar in Plymouth, and it was to him that a TINTAGEL (SX 060884) farmer went when his crops failed and his cattle fell ill, gave no milk or died. The White Witch visited very corner of the farm, with the farmer, his family and farmhands processing behind him with lighted candles. As he went, the Pellar read aloud from a book. The treatment worked: the evil was removed and the crops and cattle flourished once again.

Many Pellars wore a magical stone: the Milpreve. This took the form of a pierced bead with snake-like patterns. Historians tell us that these were beads of Egyptian faience, imported into Britain in prehistoric times. Folk-lore differs and holds that the Milpreve – the word means 'a thousand serpents' – is magically produced by masses of snakes, usually adders, coming together and joining their froth in a bubble, or hissing over a hazel-wand on which the Milpreve forms. Such massing of snakes was noted in locations in West Cornwall: BARTINNEY (SW 395294) and VELLAN-DRUCHAR MOOR (SW 424264) in particular.

Perhaps the most celebrated of all Pellars was Tamsin Blight ("Tammy Blee") of HELSTON (SW 660275). Originally hailing from Redruth, she parted from her husband, James Thomas, and went to live in Helston where she was much sought after for her wonderful powers during the mid 19th century. Reputedly descended from Lutey, stories of her astonishing talents still circulate. On one occasion, when Tamsin was still quite young, she was too ill to attend to a sick horse. Instead she touched her own young son, transferring her powers to him so that he could pass the healing spell to the horse, which was cured. Even when near the end of her life, people brought to her bedside in stretchers would leave her house unaided.

Of the various charms which were used to heal the sick, hundreds are still known. These vary from the revolting – packets of grave-earth, or a used hangman's rope, hung about the neck – to the use of herbal mixtures still used in more conventional practice today. The power of the witch, black, or white, stems from deepest prehistory; the surrounding of ourselves with modern technology does not change the fact that these beliefs and powers still linger on today.

9

Ghosts and Demons

Cornwall is a haunted place, with so many ghosts and spectres that to describe them all would take a sizeable book. Generally they fall into two categories: the harmless benign ghost, "bucca-gwidn", and the malevolent one, "bucca-du". Some are simple haunters of houses, others are spirits of coast and country.

The most famous Cornish ghost falls into the latter category; that of John Tregeagle (pron. "tr'gay-gl"). Tregeagle was a real person who hailed from TREVORDER (SW 987703) near Wadebridge, and was said to have become wealthy by dishonesty. He held the position of Steward to John, Earl of Radnor in the 17th century and was the same man who had issued the warrant for the arrest of Anne Jefferies (Chapter 2).

Versions of Tregeagle's story vary, but it would appear that, shortly before his death, he had witnessed the loan of money from one man to another. When the lender demanded repayment, the debtor denied all knowledge and so the case came to court at Bodmin Assizes. The dead Tregeagle, though, had been the only witness and the debtor, sure of his ground, declared to the court that: "If Tregeagle ever saw it, I wish to God he'd come and declare it". To his everlasting horror, the shade of the dead Steward appeared in the courtroom and, with a grin of sheer malice, told the defendant that it would not be so easy to get of him as it was to summon him.

The debtor sought the aid of the priesthood to rid him of the ghost, and they eventually bound him to the impossibly endless task of emptying DOZMARY POOL (SX 195745) with a holed limpet shell. The ghost bent to its task while the devil and his hunting pack waited for the slightest pause from work. The ghost took advantage of the fiend's inability to cross open water so, by leaping across the pool, he gained a head start and ran for ROCHE ROCK (SW 991597).

There, and with the hellish pack close behind, he dashed his head through the window of the chapel so that at least part of him was in sanctuary, but the hunters tormented his nether parts. It was not long before the poor hermit of the chapel could no longer stand the hideous head and its screaming.

The chapel remains on Roche Rock, where the restless ghost of Tregeagle sought sanctuary (C. Weatherhill)

The monks of Bodmin were brought in to deal with the troublesome ghost who, under their holy protection, was taken to PADSTOW (SW 920750) and put to the task of binding ropes of sand: an impossible task made worse by the fact that the tides invariably undid his work. His cries of anguish grew so unbearable that the good people of the area implored the monks to remove him.

His next task was to carry sacks of sand from one side of the Cober estuary to the other – and of course the daily tides would carry them back. This task ended when the devil slyly tripped the ghost, causing him to drop his full sack which spilled its load, blocking the estuary forever and forming the lake of LOE POOL (SW 646250). Now it was the turn of the townspeople of Porthleven to demand the removal of the howling spirit.

GWENVER COVE (SW 362277) was the next place to which Tregeagle was taken, again to spin ropes of sand which, as the sand here was particularly fine, was a more difficult task than before. He succeeded in this one winter by wetting the ropes with fresh water from the Vellandreath brook which, as it froze, bound them.

Finally, and to this day, Tregeagle is bound to the task of sweeping sand from PORTHCURNO (SW 388222) around the headland of Tolpedn-penwith into NANJIZAL BAY (SW 355237) and, of course, the strong currents and tides sweep it all back again. When the Atlantic storms are at their height and the winds howl and scream around the clifftop carns, the sound is held to be the anguished voice of John Tregeagle.

A 19th century engraving of Tol-pedn-penwith, close to Porthgwarra, where love extended beyond death

Close under Tol-pedn-penwith is the tiny haven of PORTHGWARRA (SW 372217), the scene of a poignant ghost story. William was a fisherman's son who worked for a rich farmer at nearby Roskestal, and who fell in love with his employer's daughter, Nancy. He often took summers off to go to sea which suited Nancy's parents who disapproved of the relationship. More than once they tried to persuade their daughter to seek someone else but she refused. In the end, her father consented to their marriage if William would first try his fortune at sea for three years, in the hope that time would dissolve their love.

He was gone for months over the three years, but Nancy's love for him had not lessened. Daily, she walked to nearby Hella Point in the hope of sighting the ship that was bringing him home, but in vain.

Then, one night, she heard William's voice under her window, entreating her to come to the cove where his boat awaited. It was time, he said, for her to be his bride. This was heard by Nancy's Aunt Prudence who followed the lovers to the cove and watched as they seemed to float over the rocks towards a small boat. Briefly, a mist veiled them from the old woman's sight and, when it cleared, boat and lovers had disappeared.

That same night, William's father had seen a vision of his son, and heard his voice bid him farewell; that he had only come to claim his bride. Neither were seen again and it was learned that William had died at sea that very day.

A very similar, but more sinister, tale is also told in West Penwith, of Nancy Trenoweth of ALSIA MILL (SW 395252) and her lover Frank Lanyon (pron. le-NINE) of BOSCEAN (SW 401233). This story resembles that of the lovers of Porthgwarra in that the parents of both were much opposed to the romance, and that Lanyon went off to see while Nancy took service at Kemyel near Mousehole. However, Nancy gave birth to a child. Like William at the Porthgwarra story, Lanyon was gone for more than three years and no word from him was heard.

On All Hallows Eve, Nancy took the fateful step of employing magic by sowing hemp and chanting: "Hemp-seed I sow thee; Hemp-seed grow thee; And he who will my true love be; Come after me and show thee". Three times the chant was made, then Nancy looked back over her left shoulder. There stood the apparition of Lanyon, but looking so enraged that she screamed, breaking the spell.

Soon after, during the November storms, a ship was wrecked under Burnewhall Cliff with the loss of nearly everyone aboard. Among those who lived was Frank Lanyon, but he was just a moment from death. He begged that Nancy be sent for, so that he could be married to her before he died.

His parents ignored his wishes and Nancy was not even informed of Lanyon's death, or of his burial at St Buryan. On the night following the funeral, Nancy was hailed by a horseman, and the voice was that of Frank Lanyon. He told her that he had just arrived home, and that he had come to make her his bride. She immediately mounted the horse behind him, but felt his helping hand to be a cold as ice. Only when the horse stopped to drink at the ford in Trewoofe Bottoms did she realise her peril, for the horseman's reflection in the water showed him to be wrapped in a shroud. Before she could react, the spectre grasped the hem of her dress in a grip of iron, and the horse broke into a wild gallop towards St Buryan. Nancy shrieked for help and the blacksmith ran from his forge and freed her by burning through the dress with a hot iron. The ghost let out an awful wail, passed over the churchyard wall and vanished on the grave of Frank Lanyon. The frantic horse, now riderless, sped through the village and was found dead the next morning on Burnewhall Cliff.

Nancy did not survive her terrible ordeal and she, too, died before morning. She was buried with Lanyon and, when the grave was opened to receive her body, the piece of her dress which had remained in the spectre's grip was found within.

It was a vengeful spirit which haunted the Jacobean lawyer Ezekiel Grosse, of ROSEWARNE (SW 646408), Camborne. Grosse (1564-1631) is notorious in history for having gained the estates of some of the richest families in Cornwall through ruthless money-lending and foreclosure. Among these was Rosewarne.

Grosse had not been long in residence at Rosewarne when the ghost of an old man appeared to him, and led him to where a fortune in gold had been buried in the grounds. Ezekiel became fabulously wealthy and, in spite of his deserved reputation, rose to the top of the social pinnacle on account of the lavish banquets he held.

The ghost had promised to return when Grosse was at his happiest, and this occurred one Christmas Eve, when the house was packed with celebrating guests. In the midst of all, the ghost appeared, fixed Grosse with a terrible stare, uttered a shriek of laughter and vanished. One by one, the frightened guests made their excuses and left, even though

Grosse tried to convince them that it had all been a lavish trick of his own.

Each party he held attracted less guests and, each time, the ghost appeared. At length, no-one would visit Rosewarne. Having raised Grosse to the heights of social grace, the ghost had, almost at a stroke, destroyed his happiness. At last, Ezekiel sought the demands of the ghost who had been one of the now defunct de Rosewarne family. He was to relinquish the ownership of Rosewarne, and pass it to his own faithful servant, John Call. After this had been accomplished, Ezekiel Grosse suffered a mysterious death and it was said that his spirit was seen being dragged over Carn Brea by a host of demons.

Suicides were much feared in Cornwall, and it was once the custom to bury such unfortunates at crossroads, where their restless spirits would be confused as to which way to go. To prevent the suicide's ghost from walking at all, it was not uncommon for a spear to be thrust through the coffin. An unimpaled suicide named Tucker, buried at a junction of three roads near WENDRON (SW 678310), solved the problem of choosing which way to go by leaping up on the back of a farmer's horse. This became a habit and Parson Jago had to be called in to put Tucker's ghost to rest.

There were a number of priests in Cornwall who were noted ghost-layers. Jago of Wendron was one, and among others were Woods of Ladock, Richards of Camborne and Dodge of TALLAND (SX 228516). The Reverend Richard Dodge was vicar at Talland from 1713-47 and his help was requested by the Reverend Mills of Lanreath in ridding the area of a spectral coach drawn by the headless horses. After fruitlessly watching the haunted stretch of road one night, they decided to try again another night. Each of the clergymen went his own way. It was Dodge's horse that warned him that something was wrong, by wheeling round and bolting back to the haunted spot at Blackadon. To his horror, Dodge saw the ghostly coach and the senseless body of Parson Mills beside it. The spectral driver suddenly uttered: "Dodge is come, I must be gone"!, leapt into the coach and drove furiously away. The Rev. Mills recovered, but no further sighting of the coach or its black-clad driver was ever made.

It was held by some that Dodge was in league with the local "fair-traders" (smugglers) and that he spread the rumours of ghosts on certain routes to ensure that people kept away from them at night.

A well recorded case of exorcism involved the ghost of BOTATHAN

(SX 295818), near South Petherwin. On a June day in 1665, Parson John Ruddle of Launceston, after preaching a funeral sermon at South Petherwin was invited by a Mr Bligh to his home at Botathan. There, a neighbouring priest told Ruddle of the Bligh's youngest son, who was haunted by a ghost he met in a nearby field. The ghost was that of Dorothy Dingley, who had died some eight years previously. Ruddle was taken to the field by the boy, saw the ghost for himself and noted that the family spaniel fled in terror at the apparition. On a further visit, Ruddle spoke with the ghost, after which it disappeared for the last time.

The most noted ghost-layer of West Cornwall was the Rev. William Polkinghorne, Vicar of Lelant and St Ives in the early 18th century. It was he who was called in to deal with one of the many ghosts of KENEGIE (SW 482326), a mansion to the north of Penzance. Now a hotel, Kenegie is one of Britain's most haunted houses, with most of its ghosts being connected with the Harris family who held it during the 17th and 18th centuries.

The troublesome ghost in question was that of a roisterous gambling, hunting and womanising man known to all as "Wild Harris" who, even after his death, refused to leave the estate. Six younger priests, believing the task of settling the ghost to be easy, found themselves in dire peril by the time Polkinghorne arrived; being trapped in Kenegie's old summerhouse by a crowd of demons, and by the shade of Wild Harris who appeared in a black, long-skirted coat and plumed sable cap.

When Polkinghorne came into the room, the ghost exclaimed: "Now, Polkinghorne, that thou art come, I must be gone". But the priest bid him stay and, in the same breath, spoke the words that expelled the demons. He held the ghost within a circle inscribed with a pentagram and bound it with a hempen cord. With the end of his riding whip, he lifted the floor-length skirt of the spirit's coat to show his fellow priests that only flames burned beneath.

Mounted on his courageous horse, Hector, Polkinghorne led the ghost of Wild Harris to the hilltop of Castle-an-dinas, passing through a tempest raised by the enraged demons. There, he bound the ghost to its task; to count the blades of grass within an area marked out in the old hill fort's inner enclosure, and to reach the same total nine times. Then and only then, could the restless spirit of Wild Harris be given peace.

One of Cornwall's saddest ghosts is the Lady with the Lantern who wanders the rocks of The Island at ST IVES (SW 520410), looking for her child who was lost in the sea during a shipwreck. The lady herself died during rescue.

Also in St Ives, the ghost of a white horse haunts Porthgwidden beach, waiting for its master, Mr Birch who, in the 19th century, failed to return from his accustomed swim. Some say that Birch himself rides the horse down Island Road to the beach.

In East Cornwall, ghostly hounds are called "lane-dogs", the best known of which is called Darley. appearing as a small, white, headless dog, he can turn black and swell to the size of a yearling calf. This is the ghost of the early 18th century eccentric Vincent Darley of Battens and is seen on the road near NORTH HILL (SX 272766) on the eastern edge of Bodmin Moor, where Darley Ford is named after him.

Two more lane-dogs are found in the same area. "Carrier" appears as a big, black retriever who travels on Saturdays from Launceston to Liskeard and back, but is most often seen near BERRIOW BRIDGE (SX 273756). He, too, is the ghost of a man.

A miner who was killed in the Marke Valley mine appears as a black dog with flaming eyes "like saucers". From the mine near UPTON CROSS (SX 280716), this nameless ghost travels the road to Rilla Mill, through Linkinhorne to STOKE CLIMSLAND (SX 361745).

The most famous type of Cornish ghost in animal form is the White Hare. This is a form favoured by young women who, after being crossed in love, have met their deaths by murder, suicide or a broken heart. In the form of the white hare, often with burning eyes, they haunt their false lover and eventually bring about his death.

A light-hearted claim states that the Devil never crossed the Tamar into Cornwall for fear of being put into a pasty. While he may not have crossed the Tamar – and after all, he experiences a little difficulty in crossing running water – he certainly entered Cornwall by other routes.

The Devil's Doorway at POLPERRO (SX 210510), a rent in the cliff face, is where he burst through from the Underworld in a fiery chariot drawn by a huge black horse which reared and planted its hoof deep into the ground, where a hoof-shaped pool remains.

Throughout Cornwall, the Wild Hunt is usually led by Old Nick, Old Artful or Old Mischief as he is often called. In many cases he hunts alone, usually with a pack of headless black hounds.

He also retains his Cornish name: the Jowle. In the Wheal Cock section of the BOTALLACK MINE sett (SW 364341), a tin-stamping mill once stood on the cliff above a deep chasm. In this building, miners often met for a game of cards. One evening, a stranger joined in the game, and won every hand. Only when his cloven foot was seen did the miners realise who the mysterious gambler had been. The mill acquired a new name, and the chasm in the cliff is still called Stamps an Jowle Zawn ("chasm of the devil's stamps").

A mile or so inland rises a lonely, weird hill topped by a strangely shaped granite tor known as CARN KENIDJACK (SW 388330): the hooting carn. Here, the devil appears as a hooded and cloaked rider on a lean black horse, hunting lost souls across the moor. At a nearby stile, he catches his prey; the forlorn spirits being unable to cross it. An ancient, sunken track leading onto this moor from the direction of Botallack is still called Devil's Lane.

Two miners were returning home to St Just from their mine near Morvah one evening. Although it was sunset, they decided to risk the shorter route past the dreaded Carn but twilight fell quicker than expected and it was gloomy by the time they neared the haunted spot. Among the rocks were flickering lights. The miners could make out large forms moving about, and heard a rough three-man's song, the chorus of which was a piercing hoot.

A horseman came up behind them. He was hooded and cloaked but told the miners he was going up to the carn to watch the wrestling, and bade them follow. Some strange force compelled them to do so. They did not know the rider, but they knew the bony black horse – it worked the whim at their own mine.

At the Carn, they found themselves among rough giants with painted faces, who formed themselves in to a circle. Two of the giants stepped forward to wrestle, and a voice called out for a light. The horseman, who had squatted on the ground drew back his hood and, as his eyes blazed with light, the miners realised that it was the Devil himself who had led them there. The wrestling was magnificent but, at length, one of the combatants lifted the other and hurled him down in a back fall, and he lay motionless.

Howling with triumph, the hellish host crowded around the victor, while the miners tended the loser. Finding that he was dying, they uttered a prayer for his soul whereupon the hill was suddenly plunged into darkness. A gale shrieked around the terrified men, then vanished and the hill was restored to moonlight. They were alone, but saw a great black cloud rolling away, out to sea, and in its midst were the two blazing eyes of the Devil. The miners could not find their way off the hill, despite knowing the ground perfectly well, and had to wait for sunrise to break the spell.

Long ago, at the other end of Cornwall, a profane priest named

Dando dwelt at ST GERMANS (SX 359578). Much given to hunting, as well as drinking, Dando's hounds had bagged him several deer and he called on his companions for a drink, even if they had to go to hell for it on the Sabbath it was. A hunter not known to Dando came forward, offering a flask of liquor "distilled in the establishment you speak of". Dando drank deeply, and its powers of intoxication worked almost immediately. Looking round, he saw that the strange hunter had taken several head of his own game. Argument and profanity got him nowhere and, in the end, Dando declared that: "I'll go to hell after them"!

A carving in St German's church records the tale of Dando and his dogs

"So you shall", replied the hunter, lifting the monk off the ground and placing Dando in front of him on the back of his coal-black horse. In the sight of everyone, the horse and its riders galloped away down Erth Hill, the hounds following close behind. When it reached the banks of the Lynher, it leapt far out into the waters of the river which, when they had closed over horse, riders and hounds, boiled for a moment. That was the last ever seen of Dando, but his story was carved into a chair in St German's Church, where it can be seen today.

The West Cornish story of "Duffy and the Devil", centred on the old mansion of TREWOOFE (SW 440253, pron. 'trove') near Lamorna Cove, finds parallels all over Europe. It is a very Cornish version of "Rumpelstiltskin", or Scotland's "Whuppity Stoorie", where Squire Lovell (properly Levelis) marries the peasant girl Duffy, in the belief that she is the finest needleworker in the west. He is unaware that the work is really that of a devil, who has offered his favour to Duffy on condition that if she cannot correctly guess his name after a three year period, then she must be his.

Duffy discovers the secret with just hours to go. The Square returns from hunting with a wild tale of having started a hare, chased it across country until it went to ground in the Fugoe Hole: an Iron Age fogou, or underground passage. Undaunted, the Squire had leapt from his horse and followed it into the dark passage which, as fogous are said to do, went on underground for a great distance (in fact, few exceed 20 metres in length). After skirting a subterranean lake, his hounds turned tail and ran back, baying in terror, and the Squire saw that a great gathering of witches was taking place around a huge fire.

Among them, the Squire recognised a local witch called Bet of the Mill, and concluded that the hare he had chased had been her. In the midst of the revelling throng was a small, black-clad man with a forked tail, and the Squire had heard him singing verses, one of which had claimed that Duffy would never guess that his name was Terrytop (or, in another version, Tarraway). Of course, Duffy faces the demon at the appointed hour, and names him, whereupon he vanishes, and all the work he had provided during the past three years dissolves. "Duffy and the Devil" became a traditional Christmas play in West Cornwall and was rewritten as such by Robert Morton Nance early in this century.

10

Sacred Waters

To the Celtic peoples, the earth represented a living entity; the Mother, sometimes called Donn or Danu, who provided them with life. Water, the most precious commodity of all, and a visible form of the life-force itself, flowed through the body of the Mother as the life-blood flows through our veins.

Little wonder, then, that lakes, rivers, streams and, above all, the wells and springs where the water sprang from the body of the Mother, were revered by our ancestors. These wells and springs were seen as possessing the powers of healing and divination, and many ancient practices concerning water live with us today. For example, when we toss a coin into a "wishing well", we are actually continuing the Iron Age tradition of offering metal objects – swords, shields, chains – to the sacred waters.

In Cornwall, as elsewhere, natural wells and springs were sought after for their powers which came from the Mother herself. Belief in their properties were such that Christianity absorbed and adopted them, rather than attempt to suppress or scorn the well-lore of the people. In this way, many ancient springs became holy wells and Cornwall alone contains more than three hundred of them.

The most powerful of them all was MADRON WELL (SW 446328), near Penzance, to which people travelled from far and wide for its great healing and oracular properties. As recently as the 19th century, this well was attended by a woman well-versed in the proper procedures: the last recorded was An' (Aunt) Katty who lived in the Bosullows three miles away. Such attendants recalled the well-priestesses of old. At this and many other wells, it was the practice of those who had come to be healed to tear a strip of cloth from their own clothing, and hang it on an overhanging tree or bush. As the cloth rotted, so the disease or illness would subside. Known in Scotland as "clooties", these strips of rag, often festooning the tree, are known as "jowds" in Cornwall. Divination was most often sought by young women eager to know their marital prospects. Crossed straws, fixed by a pin, were dropped into the well and the number of bubbles which arose foretold the number of years which would pass before marriage. Those already in love dropped pairs of pins or pebbles into the water. The future of the relationship was foretold by the objects sinking together or separating.

Children brought for healing were stripped naked, plunged three times against the sun (west to east), then dragged three times around the well in a sunwise (deosil) direction. Then, the child would be clothed, wrapped in a blanked and laid to sleep nearby white yet another jowd was added to the tree, usually the magical hawthorn.

The pagan power of Madron Well was so strong that early Christianity did not attempt to adopt it. Instead, a tiny chapel containing an alternative well was built about 100 metres away, and the water that feeds this comes from the same source as the older well. It was in this Christian well that the most famous instances of healing took place. In

the early 17th century, John Thomas and William Cork, both crippled in the legs, were cured enough for one to resume work as a fisherman and the other to serve in the Royalist army. They made three annual visits to the well on the eve of Corpus Christi (June 18). The best recorded instance of healing was that of John Trelil, who had been paralysed from the waist down since a childhood accident. Helped by a close friend, Trelil visited the well chapel on the first three Thursdays in May, each time bathing in the water and then sleeping on an artificial mound called St Madern's Bed,

The alternative Christian well at Madron, sited within an early well chapel (C. Weatherhill)

beside the chapel's altar

slab. Four years later, he was fit enough to enlist in the Royalist army. He died in battle at Lyme, Dorset, in 1644. This miraculous cure was recorded by Bishop Hall of Exeter in his "Treatise on the Invisible World" in 1640.

GULVAL WELL (SW 486317) was utterly destroyed by late Victorian redevelopment of Gulval Churchtown, and yet it was another far-famed well. Like Madron Well, it had a female attendant until as late as the 18th century. This well was not sought out for any powers of healing, but as an oracle. By signs not now remembered, it could divulge the whereabouts of stolen goods but the most common use put to the well was its ability to determine the health of absent relatives and friends. If the water bubbled up clear, the absent person was in good health; if muddy, the person was sick. Most dreaded was no reaction at all; if the water remained still, the absent person was dead.

BOSPORTHENNIS WELL (SW 439363), lost and forgotten until its rediscovery in 1991, was once reputed to have been every bit as powerful as Madron Well.

Some wells were claimed to have been miraculously formed by the actions of the saints, the early Christian priests whose names remain. ST MERIASEK'S WELL (SW 647406), Camborne, sprang from a rock which had been struck by the saint's staff. Similar origins are claimed for FENTONLUNA (SW 915755), Padstow (by St Petroc's staff) and ST MINVER WELL (SX 937764), which also possesses powers of healing, notably for whooping cough, and divination. VENTON WINEAR (SW 615388) at Roseworthy, sprang up where St Gwinear planted his elder-wood staff before being beheaded by King Teudar.

In the past, when medical knowledge was limited and the hygiene of the home fell well below modern standards, the incidence of child disease and mortality was high. Anxious mothers were provided with hope by the holy wells, a number of which were noted for being efficacious for the diseases of children.

CHAPEL EUNY WELL (SW 399289), Sancreed, was particularly famous for this, although it was considered most powerful on the first three Wednesdays of May. There are in fact two wells here, just a few metres apart. An external spring feeds the lesser well which, in turn, feeds the holy well itself through an underground channel. It cured mesenteric diseases, sores and wounds but, as was explained in Chapter 2, it failed to exorcise the spriggan's brat in the tale of "The Changeling of Brea Vean".

Blight's drawing of Jesus Well, St Minver

ALSIA WELL (SW 393251), beautifully set in a quiet valley near St Buryan, was also at its best on the first three Wednesdays of May. Weak children were treated here and, as at Madron, young women counted the bubbles from dropped pebbles to ascertain how many years would pass before they married.

MENACUDDLE WELL (SX 013535), St Austell, was also reputed to cure weak children as well as ulcers. Divination was practiced here by dropping bent pins into the water.

DUPATH WELL (SX 374693) in its large and spectacular granite building near St Dominic is big enough for total immersion. Its waters cured whooping cough.

ST NEOT WELL (SX 183681) was visited on the first three mornings of May for the treatment of weak children.

ST GUNDRED'S WELL (SW 985617) at Roche was used for general healing, but especially in the case of children. As at Madron, Alsia and other wells, girls sought divination with their bent pins and this well was thought especially powerful on Holy Thursday and the following two Thursdays. A second well exists at ROCHE ROCK (SW 991597) and was recently rediscovered. This was said to ebb and flow with the tides despite it being 200 metres above sea level and well inland. This is not a natural spring, but an artificial hole in a rock containing rainwater which evaporates in dry spells, so giving the impression of ebbing and flowing.

Blight's drawing of Menacuddle Well

CUBERT has two holy wells. The first is near Trevornick (SW 773588); the second is truly magical, consisting of a series of natural basins in a cavern at Holywell Bay (SW 764602), which is only accessible at low water. Both wells were sought after to cure children's diseases and deformities, as well as bowel conditions. At the cave well, the patient was passed through a natural aperture in the rock and cripples were known to have left their crutches behind after seeking the well's powers.

Madness was treated at ST NONNA'S WELL (SX 226816), Altarnun, by the method known as bowssening. The patient would be seated on the wall surrounding the well and tumbled into the water by a blow on the chest. There, a group of people would repeatedly dip him until his fury had abated. The bowssening pool has gone, but the well remains.

Blight's drawing of Dupath Well

The restored well of ST CLEER (SX 249683) was also a bowssening well, where the insane were immersed in the pool beside the well.

Diseases of the eye were also common in past centuries. In the Penwith peninsula, cures were sought at CASTLE HORNECK WELL (SW 463302), and especially at COLLURIAN WELL (SW 523347). Here the place-name does not appear to be Cornish, but the Greek KOL-LORION, "eye-salve". Other wells noted for the treatment of eye complaints included ST JAMES'S WELL, St Breward (SX 091769); VIN-CENT'S WELL (SW 673381) at Bolenowe near Camborne; JOAN'S PIT-CHER WELL, Lewannick (SX 285810); THE WELL OF OUR LADY OF NANCE at Colan (SW 870604); ST PETER'S WELL, Polperro (SX 200510) which had to be visited on three successive mornings before sunrise; and

ST LEVAN'S WELL (SW 381218), which was also reputed to cure toothache.

The natural basins within the cave at Holywell Bay (P. Devereux)

ST EUNY'S WELL (SW 691413) at Redruth had the power of ensuring that no-one was baptised in its waters would hang. The same power belonged to the now covered over LUDGVAN WELL (SW 503331), which also cured speech and eye problems before an exorcised demon spat in it. Nevertheless, it retained its power of immunity from the hangman's noose. Local faith in the well's ability was shaken when parishioner Sarah Polgrean was hanged for the murder of her husband, but was restored when it was discovered that she had been baptised in a neighbouring parish.

The water of ST KEYNE'S WELL (SX 248603) granted domestic domination to whichever of a newly-wed couple was first to drink it. Robert Southey immortalised this well in a poem which described how, after a marriage service, the groom bolted from the church, frantic to be the first to drink from the well. The bride calmly watched, producing a bottle of well water she'd taken to church with her ...

Blight's drawing of St Cleer well, before its restoration.

Another curious property belonged to ST ISSEY WELL (SW 938697), which cleansed the conscience.

In the Isles of Scilly, the islanders of St Agnes dropped pins into the waters of ST WARNA'S WELL (SV 881078), in the hope that its power would drive a ship onto their shores, so that its timber and cargo would help them through the winter.

ST JULIOT WELL (SX 133913) treated skin diseases, and ST CADOC'S WELL (SW 885749) near Harlyn Bay was sought after by those who suffered from abdominal ailments.

Wells which had a reputation for general healing include: LADY WELL (SX 009467) and BRASS WELL (SX 009457), both at Mevagissey; ST ANN'S WELL, Hessenford (SX 313575); THE PIPE WELL in the centre of Liskeard (SX 252645) which, although its water is now condemned because it issues from four lead pipes, also gave matrimonial happiness; ST PEDYR'S WELL, Treloy (SW 858623); PHILLACK WELL (SW 565384), before its powers were curtailed by having a mangy dog washed in it in 1720; ST BERNARD'S WELL, St Stephen in Brannel (SW 963558); ST WENN'S WELL (SW 955642); and ST NUN'S WELL, Pelynt (SX 224564).

Blight's drawing of St Keyne's well

There is a modern tendency for holy wells – notably Madron Well – to be referred to, and somewhat downgraded, as "wishing wells". However, the only Cornish well which would seem to have been purely used as a wishing well is VENTON UNY (SW 536387), alternatively called the Fairy Well, in a cliffside nutgrove near Lelant.

The power of St Warna's well was invoked by those who desired that a ship be wrecked on the island of St Agnes (P. Devereux)

On the hill of Carnmarth, above Redruth, is FIGGY DOWDY'S WELL (SW 715406), the nickname having been that of a past landowner. Local children used to chant that: "Figgy Dowdy had a well; On the top of Carnmarth Hill; He kept it locked both night and day; Lest folk should take his water away". It was also known as Margery Daw's Well, the only known place where this obscure saint, who was taken away by the Small People in punishment for her slovenly ways, is referred to. On Good Friday mornings, children would perform the curious ritual of taking their dolls to Figgy Dowdy's Well to be baptised.

The same ritual took place at a lonely well near Carn Galva; now identified as the recently rediscovered VENTON BEBIBELL (SW 430352), the name of which would, interestingly, appear to mean "well of the little people".

Larger expanses of water were also associated with ancient beliefs. The weird DOZMARY POOL (SX 194745) in the middle of Bodmin Moor was believed to be bottomless; a symbolic entrance to the underworld. Cornwall's only other natural freshwater lake, LOE POOL (SW 648250) shares with other waters, such as the River Dart, the claiming of a life every seven years.

11

Lost Lands

Legends of ancient inundations exist in almost every culture in the world. In the Pacific, Polynesian lore tells of the lost continent of Mu while closer to home, the sunken land of Atlantis was first recorded by Pliny. The Bible features the great flood survived by Noah, and even the "Arabian Nights" speaks of sunken lands.

The Celtic countries, and particularly the Brittonic lands, are no exceptions. Wales has its lost cantref of Gwaelod Garanhir beneath the waters of Cardigan Bay, while Brittany has the sunken city of Caer Ys. Cornwall, too has its drowned land, Lyonesse, but Cornish legend adds an additional dimension; tracts and cities lost on dry land.

PENHALE SANDS (SW 769565) is a vast tract of huge sand-dunes ("towans") stretching from Perranporth to Holywell, extending for as much as a mile inland and reaching a height of 85 metres. These and other large areas of towan on the Cornish coast apparently began to form during the Early Christian period (c.400 – 1000 AD). Local legend tells that a great city, called Langarrow or Langona, once extended across this entire area. It contained seven churches, each remarkable for its beauty and size, and its wealthy inhabitants drew their living from farming, fishing and mining. The elders resolved to transform the Gannel estuary into a harbour, dredging it clear of sand so that sizeable ships could sail well inland, and convicts from all over Britain were brought in as workers. These were made to live well away from the city, in rough huts and caves. Even so, and after a long period of time, the citizens and the convicts began to mingle and even to intermarry, the result being that the moral standards of the city sank irreversibly into deep decline. Like the Biblical cities of Sodom and Gomorrah, divine retribution descended on Langarrow. This took the shape of a severe gale which blew without interruption for three days and nights. The sea washed up huge quantities of sand which was the blown inland, covering the city of Langarrow and its inhabitants forever.

The northern boundary of the Penhale Sands is a stream beyond which the sands never spread, and just to the north of the stream is the hamlet of ELLENGLAZE (SW 776578). This is said to have been its fourth site; the others having been closer to the sea until each in turn was inundated by sand. A young lord was responsible for building on the present site in spite of learned warnings that the new settlement would suffer the same fate as the others. He ignored them and, when the house was finished, he rode off to the Lizard peninsula to fetch his bride. On his return, he found his retinue anxiously watching the ominous movement of the sandhills as a gale blew in from the sea. They claimed that a curse had been laid on the land and a search was made for a scapegoat. An old woman found hiding in a barn was dragged before the lord and his wife to face charges of witchcraft. The lord ordered that she should hang, but his bride begged him to spare the old woman's life. The lord compromised, saying that if, by nightfall, the sands had ceased to threaten the house, then the woman would live. If not, she would die. At nightfall it was seen that the sands were still moving. The young bride implored the old woman to reverse the spell if she could, but the crone swore that she was innocent. "Then the saints save us all" said the bride, and she planted a kiss on the old woman's cheek: the kiss freely given that breaks the bonds of magic that bind a witch. A witch cannot shed tears, but the kiss caused tears to well from the old woman's eyes. These, as they fell to the ground, formed the stream of water which flows to this day, so saving Ellenglaze forever from the sands.

The Penhale Sands were the site of the early religious settlement of Lanpiran, and in the 19th century, the sand-dunes shifted to reveal the 8th century chapel of St Piran, probably standing on an older site, and its surrounding graveyard. This had been overwhelmed in pre-Norman times, causing a second church to be built 400 metres further inland. This was overwhelmed by the sand in 1804 and the third church was built at Perranzabuloe, over two miles to the south and well away from the creeping sands. The 9th century church was reburied in 1981, to secure it from the twin threats of flooding and vandalism.

Similarly, a 19th century shifting of sand-dunes at GWITHIAN (SW 588418) revealed another early church but this was reclaimed by the sand. There is another tradition here of a buried town, Conetconia or Connerton.

To the south west, the towans at LELANT (SW 547380) and PHIL-LACK (SW 562387), on either side of the Hayle estuary, cover what is said to have been meadow land swallowed in a single night. The original church and village of Lelant are said to lie under the waters of St Ives Bay. The towans at Phillack cover Riviere, the castle of King Teudar, persecutor of the Irish saints led by Gwinear, who landed in St Ives Bay (see Chapter 3). W. H. Pascoe's recent book "Teudar – A King of Cornwall" details the legends of this man and the saints he hounded, and also provides intriguing evidence which might pinpoint the actual site of Riviere.

It is the ever-present sea which generally covers lost lands and some of these were real. Chapel Rock at PERRANPORTH (SW 754546), on which once stood Chapel-an-Garder, is now an isolated stack surrounded by the sea at high water but it was once large enough to have included a graveyard. The curious arches in the stacks off the cliff to the south of the rock have been formed from the levels and adits of the old Droskyn Mine, showing just how quickly erosion has set in on this coast. Further traditions speak of an area landward of a line between the Bawden Rocks (SW 701533) and Carter's Rock (SW 754594) having once been dry land, destroyed by a series of storms.

Submerged forests can be traced at various points around the Cornish coast at extreme low waters; at Bude, the mouth of the Camel, St Columb Porth, Perranporth, Portreath, the mouth of the Hayle, Praa Sands, Porthleven, the mouth of the Helford River, Maenporth, Restronguet Creek, Gerrans Bay, Fowey and Looe. These were almost certainly drowned during the same era, and at the same time as the best known of them all in Mount's Bay.

The old Cornish name for ST MICHAEL'S MOUNT (SW 515300) was "Carack Looez en Cooz" (Grey Rock in the Wood) and indeed at one time it rose from a low-lying forest of predominently oak, hazel and elder which finally succumbed to the sea at the end of the Neolithic era, c.2500 – 200 BC. Local belief claims that this forest stretched as far out as a line drawn from Cudden Point to Mousehole and that the area of water off Newlyn harbour called Gwavas Lake was truly the site of a lake within the forest, although it has to be said that soundings do not support this.

The Mount's Bay forest was also supposed to be a part of Cornwall's most famous lost land, LYONESSE, though, again, the Admiralty charts make it difficult to see how the two could have been connected. Lyonesse, according to the most enduring traditions, stretched from Land's End to the Isles of Scilly, which represent the tops of a hill range. All too many books make the mistake of claiming that the destruction of the Lyonesse was recorded in the Anglo-Saxon Chronicle's entry for the year 1099. In fact, it does no such thing. What it does say is "1099: This year, at Martinmas, the great sea-flood came up and did so much harm that no man remembered its like before". No location is specified but, as it is much more concerned with south-eastern Britain, this entry may be recording the destruction of lands in the place now occupied by the Goodwin Sands off Kent.

The lost land of Lyonesse remains one of Cornwall's strongest traditions and may well be an exaggerated memory of a real event. Now it is recalled as lying beneath the 28 miles of treacherous sea between the Scillies and the mainland. Its capital, the City of Lions, was said to have been built around the former hill which is now the dangerous reef called the Seven Stones, 16 miles WSW of Land's End and the graveyard of many a wreck, most notably the infamous Torrey Canyon (1967). Fishermen, who were said to have trawled up evidence of former buildings at this spot, called the area between the Stones "Trigva" (dwelling). The Cornish name for the reef is "Lethowsow" (milky ones) and this is sometimes cited as an alternative name for the Lyonesse itself. Lyonesse is first mentioned by the Arab geographer Idrisi in 1153 as "Dns", a probable misprint of "Lyns". This would suggest that the original pronunciation of the name was "Lee-an-ez", rather than the "Lioness" most often used today, and there is one intriguing theory that this might have represented a former "Lugh-enes" (island of the god Lugh, who appears to have had a firm place in West Cornwall's mythology).

Lyonesse was said to have been a fertile land with 140 churches. Medieval Arthurian writers made it the birthplace of Tristan, who is more likely to have hailed from Leonois in Brittany. The land was drowned in a single cataclysmic night, with only one survivor. Legends vary on who this was: a Trevelyan whose fleet white horse carried him to Perranuthnoe on Mount's Bay; a Vyvyan whose descendants settled at St Buryan and later moved to Trelowarren on the Lizard peninsula, and who was also carried to safety by a white horse; or a Lord of Goonhilly who founded Chapel Idne (narrow chapel) at Sennen Cove in thanks for his deliverance. The Trevelyan coat-of-arms features a white horse emerging from the sea, while that of the Vyvyans is surmounted by a saddled white horse. it was said that the Vyvyans always kept a similar horse in their stables, saddled ready for an emergency. The motif of the escaping lord is also found in the Breton story of the drowning of Caer Ys, where King Gradlon escapes the flood on horseback, though losing his daughter to the sea on the way.

The Reverend H. J. Whitfeld published a somewhat embellished collection entitled "Scilly and its Legends" in 1852, which contained an Arthurian tale of the destruction of Lyonesse; curious in that it is the only account to assert that the traitor Mordred survived the fateful Battle of Camlann which claimed Arthur himself.

After the battle, he pursued the few survivors of Arthur's men through Cornwall and into the Lyonesse itself. In the middle of that land, a strange cloud that had travelled ahead of Mordred's army transformed itself into the ghost of Merlin, who immediately uttered the terrible spell which plunged the doomed land and the traitor beneath the sea forever. The pitiful remainder of Arthur's men, safe on the hilltops which from that moment became the Isles of Scilly, founded a religious house on what is now Tresco in thanks for their deliverance.

The origin of the legend of Lyonesse must, to a certain extent, stem from ancient folk-memories of the Neolithic inundations of areas around the Cornish coast, particularly Mount's Bay, but more especially from the history of the Isles of Scilly themselves.

The Eastern Isles of Scilly, formerly "Goonhily" (C. Weatherhill)

Throughout the prehistoric period, this group of over a hundred islands and islets consisted of a single large island with a smaller one to the south-west. It is believed that the larger one, which included the present islands of St Mary's, Samson, Bryher, Tresco, St Martin's and the Eastern Isles, bore the name Ennor – "the land", which can be equated with the largest of the Orkneys and Shetlands which both go by the name of "Mainland". The smaller island, now St Agnes, Annet and the Western Rocks, may have been called Ek-enes ("off-island"), now corrupted to "St" Agnes. Collectively, the group was Sillina, possibly derived from the Celtic goddess Sulis, "the watcher".

Ennor consisted of low hills surrounding a central valley plain which, in Neolithic times, was wooded. Barriers of sand-dunes protected this central area from the sea but, over the centuries, they were repeatedly breached by marine surges. Substantial remains of these dune systems still survive, though submerged and the gradual sinking of the island group is still measurable.

In Roman times, the island of Ennor was still essentially intact. Its principal harbour was a deep water inlet between St Martin's and Nornour, one of the Eastern Isles, and a settlement founded on Nornour during the Bronze Age contained a building adapted in Romano-British times to a mariner's shrine. A "Vestaeum", a navigation beacon visible from the mainland, shone from the heights of St Martin's Head, and the Roman name for Land's End, Antivestaeum, "opposite the beacon" reflects this. Interestingly, the local Celtic name for Land's End during the Iron Age was Belerion, "shining one", perhaps referring to a corresponding beacon on the mainland.

At this point, it is worth remembering the Lord of Goonhilly, who owned a substantial piece of Lyonesse, and who escaped the final flood, landing at Sennen Cove and founding a chapel. Goonhilly ("hunting downs") is a tract of heathland on the Lizard peninsula and almost certainly unconnected with this legend, but it is very similar to the name Goonhily ("salt-water downs") which was apparently once applied to the area of Ennor now occupied by the Eastern Isles, one of which is still called Ganilly. To complete the jigsaw, the old name of Sennen Cove was Porth Goonhilly ("harbour for Goonhily"), indicating that it was the principal mainland harbour serving the old Sillina in ancient times.

The final insurgence of the sea which divided the islands probably occurred in the post-Roman centuries (and the waters of Crow Sound, the original central valley, have only been navigable by vessels of any size since Tudor times), which ties in quite well with the Arthurian link. This link, in turn, was strengthened by historically quite feasible legends of an Arthurian battle centred around Sennen Cove. As if to underline the connection, three of the Scillonian Eastern Isles are named Great, Middle and Little Arthur.

The legend of the lost land of Lyonesse is a wonderful illustration of how legends have grown from basic historical facts, and how they should never be discounted as pure fantasy especially when they stem from a culture such as the Cornish which has survived intact from prehistory to the present day.

12

Legends of the Sea

Nowhere in Cornwall is it possible to be more than 15 miles from the sea. With a coastline 300 miles long, and 100 miles of navigable estuaries, it is not difficult to see that the sea has always played a major part in the life of its people. Sadly the last hundred years have seen the Cornish maritime way of life decline to a shadow of its former self. The great fishing fleets which crammed every port have gone, and not even those which remain at places like Newlyn and Looe can compare with them. The fishing stations in remote coves like The Gazick and Treen have long been silent.

Since prehistoric times, Cornwall's central position in the Atlantic arc of Europe has been of paramount importance to its economy, and her mariners have braved the awesome forces of the Atlantic with incomparable courage; as most recently demonstrated by the crew of the Penlee lifeboat who never came back one black, wild night in December 1981. In spite of the economic ravages of the 20th century, their tradition, and their traditions, remain.

The name of the sea god of the ancient Cornish has not survived, but he is remembered in the form of the Bucca, to whom the fishermen of Mousehole and Newlyn left portions of their catch well into the 19th century.

It is possible that at least some of Cornwall's mermaids may have originated as marine goddesses and by far the most famous of these is the Mermaid of ZENNOR (SW 454385). For along time, a strange and beautiful woman was given to attending occasional services at the churches of Morvah and Zennor. To local people, her identity continued to be a total mystery and it was remarked that, as the years passed, she showed no sign of ageing.

Herself a beautiful singer, she became infatuated with the singing of Zennor chorister Matthew Trewhella and, after one service, he was seen accompanying her away from the church and in the direction of the cliffs. Neither were seen again.

Penberth Cove, one of the last of the traditional fishing coves (C. Weatherhill)

It was only when, a few years later, a ship's captain described how he'd anchored in Pendour Cove only to be hailed by a "merrymaid" who complained that his anchor was blocking entry to her home, that the stunned parishioners of Zennor realised what had happened to "Mathey" Trewhella, and the true identity of the mysterious woman. it appears that she was a limited shape-shifter, able to have legs for her forays on to dry land but it is in her more accustomed shape that she appears on the bench-end carving that exists in Zennor church to this day.

A mermaid who was less friendly to shipping once frequented the

Half Tide Rock (formerly the Mermaid's Rock) off LAMORNA COVE (SW 455239). Her magnetic singing was always at its most plaintive before a wreck, and shore-bound spirits were said to echo her in low, moaning voices. Lured by the song, young men often swam out to the rock, never to return. This deadly creature much resembles the Sirens of the Odyssey.

The Mermaid of Zennor (old postcard)

A 19th century engraving of Lamorna Cove

At PADSTOW (SW 920750), the terrible Doom Bar, the great sandbank which blocks the mouth of the Camel estuary, formed as a result of a mermaid's curse. A story is told of a young Padstow fisherman who saw a woman sitting on a rock by a pool. She sat with her back to him, absently combing her abundant and extremely long hair. Boldly, the young man walked up to her and spoke. When she turned, he saw to his horror that she was a mermaid and his first instinct was to shoot this terrible creature. The wound was mortal and, as she died, she spoke a curse on the port. Overnight, in a mighty storm, the Doom Bar formed and the horrified people of Padstow found the next morning that it had already claimed a number of ships and lives – as it has ever since.

On Cornwall's south coast, the port of SEATON (SX 303543) was similarly overwhelmed by sand after a local seaman had injured a mermaid.

Robert Hunt tells the story of an old man of CURY (SW 678213) and a mermaid, but William Bottrell's older and fuller version makes it clear that the man in question was under thirty, hailed from near the LIZARD (SW 700116), and was named Lutey. Walking on a beach one summer's evening, he heard a mournful cry and found a mermaid stranded in a pool by the outgoing tide. On being carried back to the sea by Lutey, the mermaid Morvena gave him a golden comb with a pearl handle, telling him that if ever he needed her guidance, he should comb the water three times, calling her name each time, and she would come. For his kindness, she granted him three wishes. Lutey wanted nothing of wealth, but chose the ability to break the spells of witchcraft; to have power over spirits so as to compel them to tell him all he should need to know for the benefit of others; and that these gifts should remain in his family for ever. Being a faithful married man, he resisted her attempts to lure him into the water with her but she promised that, in nine years, she would come to claim him.

The wishes were granted. Lutey became a noted pellar, or white witch who could counter bewitchments and heal the sick. From him were descended the famous pellars of the Lizard peninsula, including the most famous of them all, Tamsin Blight of Helston.

Nine years to the day after his encounter with the mermaid, Lutey was out fishing with a friend on a clear moonlit night. Suddenly the mermaid appeared. Resignedly, Lutey murmured: "My hour is come", then plunged over the side to sink into the depths with the mermaid. His body was never found.

Hunt relates a tale set at PERRANPORTH (SW 756543), although he says that it is found at a number of places on the north Cornish coast. Called "The Mermaid's Vengeance" and wonderfully Gothic in style, it concerns a girl called Selina Penaluna who, when very young, had leapt from her mother's arms into a deep rock pool, to emerge more beautiful than ever. Old women declared her to be a changeling.

When she was eighteen, the young Walter Trewoofe came into her life and, as the romance blossomed, so her father's old enemy, Tom Chenalls, plotted their ruin, and the separation of father and daughter which would bring this about. He succeeded in having Selina's father sent to put to right one of his employer's ailing farms near Land's End. As Chenalls knew, Trewoofe was a man of fickle heart who suddenly disappeared to the lures of the city. The pregnant Selina pined, sickened and, as her child entered the world, died.

From that day, a succession of mishaps dogged the life of Tom Chenalls who descended into a life of drunken debauchery. Trewoofe returned, to be easily drawn into Chenalls' circle.

Then, one night, Trewoofe, the worse for drink, wandered onto the beach where he was met at the mouth of a cave by a beautiful woman, whose face was so like that of Selina, and who sang of betrayal and of her child, lying in an earth-grave, never to return to the ocean. After that encounter, Trewoofe found himself overwhelmed by remorse, depression and a secret longing to return to the cave. At last, he found the courage to do so, and, forgetful of the fact that it was the anniversary of Selina's death, met again with the woman. She kissed him: kisses on land, she told him, were false. Men kissed earth-born maidens to betray them, whereas hers was the kiss of a sea-child: the seal of constancy. He was hers until death.

The sea rose around Trewoofe as the mermaid held him in an unbreakable grip, and a great storm arose. He saw Chenalls's cottage and its drunken occupants blasted by lightening, heard his own death-chant sung by a host of sea-people who tossed his dying form from one to the other as they avenged their adopted child, Selina.

On the Isles of Scilly, the deep cave of PIPER'S HOLE (SV 888165) on Tresco, with its deep subterranean pool, is said to be the home of mermaids.

SENNEN COVE (SW 351263) retains the traditions of a unique spirit of the sea: a guardian known as the Hooper. This took the form of a fog bank which formed over the Cowloe Rocks and slowly spread out across the bay like a barrier. It emitted loud whooping sounds, hence its name, and, at night, a glow could be seen in its midst, accompanied by rising and falling showers of glowing sparks. This warned of approaching storms (see Chapter 6).

At times, and always during bad weather, the voices of the drowned are heard above the storm, hailing their own names. Another tradition, found not only around the Cornish coast but in other Celtic lands, is that of the sea calling in its debts. On a wild night, a clear voice is heard, calling three times: "The hour is come, but not the man!" Then a figure is seen on shore, rushing over the sands and into the sea, never to be seen again.

On December 18, 1811, the Scillonian brig "Aurora" was wrecked on the Land's End coast. Her master, Captain Richard Wetherall, himself from Scilly, lost his life and was laid to rest in ST LEVAN churchyard (SW 381222) where his tombstone can still be seen. It was said that, as he went down with his stricken vessel, he sounded eight bells. Those same eight bells are said to issue from the grave, signifying to any who hear it that their own life's "watch" is over.

Mariners are probably the world's most superstitious breed of men, and it is hardly surprising when they daily pit themselves against the world's most powerful and unpredictable element. Cornish fishermen are far from being an exception, and have distinct taboos. Land animals must never be mentioned by their usual name, not only on shipboard, but anywhere within hearing distance of the boat. There are a whole series of alternative names, similar to those used by miners who share the taboo (see Chapter 5), but any quadruped is a "two-decker" or "four-legger". With animals playing a special role in Celtic belief, this is probably of early origin; perhaps even prehistoric. Another set of Cornish maritime taboos is also ancient, dating back to the dawn of Christianity in these islands, and its struggle to overcome pagan Celtic religions; there must be no mention of the Christian church or clergy. Where a church-tower is used as a navigation mark, it is called a "cleeta" (Late Cornish "bell-house"), and a priest is a "fore-and-after" or "white choker". "Steeple" for St Hilary church, and "tower" for the churches of Paul and St Buryan, were considered acceptable.

Phantom ships play a significant part in Cornish maritime lore. "Jack Harry's lights", named after a St Ives man who was the first to be taken in by them, are dismissed by the sceptics as St Elmo's fire. Their view is dismissed with equal contempt by hardened seamen, especially around St Ives Bay. Take, for example, the case of the schooner which was seen in trouble off ST IVES (SW 518405). Pilot gigs were launched, rowing swiftly out to the vessel which, although it was night, was clearly visible, as was a bright light over her bow. As the first gig pulled alongside, one of its crew leapt up to grasp the schooner's bulwarks – but there was nothing solid there. As the gig crew hauled their mate back into the boat, the schooner and the light vanished. The next morning, it was found that an identical schooner, the "Neptune" of London, had been wrecked at Gwithian, on the far side of the bay, with the loss of all on board.

On one other occasion, a St Ives pilot gig went to the assistance of a large ship in the bay but, as it drew near, the ship vanished and reappeared in a position nearly three miles away. The gig tried again, with similar results, before giving it up for "Jack Harry's lights".

On a moonlit night, with a thin intermittent drizzle, another St Ives crew found themselves accompanied by a phantom ship, which remained alongside for miles. Several forms were seen to move around on her deck, but there was no response to hailing. Then, the ship vanished.

Many of these phantom ships foretold a wreck, and the stricken ship always closely resembled the ghost. Others were merely tokens of ill-omen, and the strangest of these is the phantom lugger which sails the waters of CROFT PASCO POOL (SW 732198), a small, shallow tarn on Goonhilly Downs.

Phantom ships were once held to be warning of an enemy raid; the number of ships seen foretelling the number of ships in the hostile fleet. In later times, they became a general token of ill-omen.

Porthcurno, the haunt of a phantom ship (C. Weatherhill)

The ghost ship of PORTHCURNO (SW 388223) is probably the best known of them all. An extremely old tradition, the current version is said to have originated in the 18th century when the farm of Chegwidden, a mile inland, was occupied by a particular family: a brutal old sot of a father with a young, but spiteful, second wife. The eldest son, by the first marriage, and sick of his treatment at the hands of his father and a stepmother younger than he was ran away to sea and vowed never to return until a certain member of the household was dead. He was not seen again for many years, during which time, all in the house died. With the son presumed dead, Chegwidden passed to a young relative and his teenage sister, Eleanor.

At length, the son, Martin T-, returned. Accompanied by a dark-skinned comrade and several heavy chests, he was dropped off at Porthcurno by a passing ship. He allowed the young relative and his sister to remain, saying he'd be happy just to stay there for a while. Martin – who became known simply as the Captain, and his foreign companion Jose, took to heavy drinking, wild hunting and spending money and gold like water. He built a half-decked boat which was kept at Portchcurno and in which he and Jose would take to sea, often in the wildest weather, for weeks on end. It was rumoured that they were pirates and most avoided them, apart from Eleanor, who seemed to understand them and who was decked out with expensive clothes and jewellery by the strange pair.

At length, the time for Martin's death drew near. He made Jose and Eleanor swear that, when the time came, they would take him out to die and be interred at sea, but his death was sudden. Curiously, a weighted coffin purporting to contain his body, was laid in St Levan churchyard while Jose was seen dragging heavy boxes on board the boat. One of these, they said, was sure to have held the body of Martin T-. Jose, Eleanor and Martin's favourite dog put to sea, and they were less than a league offshore when a tremendous storm blew up. It lasted for nearly a week, choking Porthcurno with so much sand that it has never been possible to keep a boat there since.

That was the last that anyone ever saw of Jose and Eleanor but, no sooner had the storm abated than an apparition of the barque was seen sailing into Porthcurno, as she has many times since. Usually she is mist-shrouded, but sometimes a glimpse of her deck reveals the shadowy forms of two men, a woman and a dog. Some say she tows a small boat behind her, but all agree that, when she reaches the shore-line, the barque takes to the land, her keel skimming smoothly over the ground. She sails up the valley to Chegwidden, hovers over the "townplace", then bears away to a croft where she vanishes near a rock under which a large hoard of foreign coins was reputedly found.

Another version of the supernatural ship – the death ship – occurs in the tale of a wrecker who dwelt at TREGESEAL (SW 373318) near St Just. It should be said here that visitors to Cornwall are assailed with stories of how Cornish wreckers lured ships onto the rocks with false lights on the cliffs. This is an invention of Victorian novelists which has been flogged to death by the tourist industry. The fact is, that such a thing never happened in recorded history, and only once in legend – and the wrecker concerned was not of local origin. In Cornwall, wrecking consisted (and still consists) of stripping a wrecked vessel of all useful articles. Until the advent of navigational aids, ships crashed onto the rock-girt Cornish shores with monotonous regularity and even in today's technological era, all too many ships and sailors end their lives on Cornwall's savage coast.

Our wrecker was a man of such evil that even his piratical colleagues could no longer stomach him so, as they passed the western tip of Cornwall, they trussed him up, rowed him into Priest Cove under Cape Cornwall, untied him and forced him ashore at gunpoint.

He bought a small farm near Tregeseal and, as time wore on, local people began to wonder why so many vessels became wrecked on the cliff bordering his holding. To their horror, they discovered that on winter nights, he was driving a horse along the clifftop, with a lantern hung from its neck and its head hobbled to a foreleg so that the movement of the light would resemble that of a ship's stern light. Any of the crews of these unfortunate ships who survived long enough to reach the shore would meet a wicked death by way of the old wrecker's axe.

At length, death and the devil came for the wrecker. His dying hours were dreadful and when local priests were sent for, they found the fiend in the room but could only exorcise him to the size and shape of a blow-fly. The room was filled with the sound of a rushing sea and the terrified screams of the dying man, calling for the priests to save him from the devils and the sailors who had come to tear him to pieces.

At that moment, men working at the harvest heard a voice from the sea calling, "The hour is come but the man isn't come"! and saw a black-rigged ship with all sail set and no-one on deck, bearing in against both wind and tide. It came right in under the cliffs and vanished into the dense black clouds which seemed to exude from her and wrap themselves around the dying wrecker's house. There, at the moment of death, the clouds rolled back to the death ship which sailed away into the distance amid a blaze of lightning.

The villagers quickly placed the wrecker's body in a coffin and sealed the lid against the ghastly expression on the dead man's face. As the coffin was borne towards the churchyard, a black pig followed the bearers – who declared that the coffin was too light to hold a body. The sky darkened and gave way to a thunderstorm with so many flashes of lightning that the bearers dropped the coffin on the churchyard stile and fled into the church for shelter. From the porch they saw the coffin burst into flame, to be whirled away into the air and, when the storm died away, all that was left were the handles and a few nails.

There are many similarities between this story and that of Cruel Coppinger, a story based at the opposite end of Cornwall, at MORWEN-STOW (SS 205153), David Coppinger, a semi-legendary character, was reputed to have been a Dane who, when his ship was inextricably driven into Harty Race during a storm, dived overboard and battled his way to shore. There he encountered a young local woman, Dinah Hamlyn, and forced her to take him up on her horse and give him shelter. He remained at her house and, when her father died, he married her.

Coppinger founded a fearsome gang of smugglers and a reign of terror. Most of his maritime activities were carried out on his ship "The Black Prince". He not only opposed the Revenue men but other bands of smugglers as well. A tale is told of a running battle in St Ives Bay between "The Black Prince" and a vessel belonging to the most famous smuggler of them all, John Carter, the "King of Prussia Cove". The wickedness of Coppinger's activities appalled the local people and, when Dinah gave birth to an imbecilic son, they held that he had inherited his father's evil and had been born without a soul.

Coppinger's cronies were finally defeated, and many killed, in a showdown with the Revenue men. Coppinger himself escaped. During a storm, a ship hove-to off Harty Pool and lowered a boat which fought its way to shore where Coppinger waited, brandishing a cutlass and cursing. He boarded the boat which took him out to the ship, and the vessel sailed away into the teeth of the storm. Cruel Coppinger never returned.

Cornish smugglers did not call themselves by that name. They were "fair-traders" whose fear of the power and spirits of the deep was equal to the courage they displayed in their constant battles against it, and against the officers of the law.

One fair-trader, a farmer from MULLION (SW 680192), was forced to miss a trip to Newlyn in a boat laden with ankers of spirits, due to an appointment in Helston. He returned late that evening to declare in sorrow: "The boat and all on board are lost". He explained that as he passed over Halzaphron Cliff, he passed his silent colleagues with their hair and clothes all dripping wet and read this as a token of their deaths at sea. He was right. The boat and crew had indeed been lost.

Cornish stories and beliefs about the sea are many. Strange things happen on that wildest of elements and will continue to do so. Even in the cold-hearted late twentieth century and in the future will tales such as these spring up, reminding us that man will never be master of "the old grey widow-maker".

13

Monumental Mysteries

There are few places in Cornwall where it is not possible to walk hand-in-hand with the past – not just the past of a few centuries ago, but of millenia. The Duchy contains more archaeological sites than any other comparable area of Britain and officialdom has only recently begun to recognise what the people have always known – that there are a great number of archaeological landscapes into which the individual monuments fit like pieces in a jigsaw to complete entire and cohesive scenes of settlements, field patterns, megaliths, forts and so on.

Of these sites and monuments, the most awesome are the megaliths: the dolmens, cairns, circles and menhirs, all built of massive stones and representing supreme feats of prehistoric engineering. Some of the hill forts and cliff castles, too, include massive stonework and it is hardly surprising that these are not only part of our social heritage but also of our legendary and mythogical heritage. Today, even the narrowest of minds are beginning to open, and professional archaeologists now speak openly of the peculiar atmosphere which envelops and exudes from these great monuments of the distant past.

The early chapters of this book describe how many of these monuments are inhabited in legend by otherworldly beings: giants, spriggans, small people. Tales such as the spriggans of Trencrom, and the belief that evil cannot enter forts such as Caer Brane where the Small People dwell, are a clear indication that these ancient sites possess guardian spirits. This is not just the case with monuments which have been known for centuries, but even those discovered in more recent times. One such case is the great and unique multi-phase stone cairn called the BALLOWALL, or CARN CLOOSE, BARROW (SW 356312), on the edge of the cliffs west of St Just. Although only discovered in the 1870s, after being buried under a pile of mining waste, miners reported seeing the small people and their lights dancing around it at night.

A number of monuments are reputed to have peculiar powers. Of the huge dolmen called ZENNOR QUOIT (SW 469380) it was said that if any of its stones were removed from the hill, they would find their own way back into place by the following morning.

At the holy well of ST CLEER (SX 249683), and during restoration in 1864, stones which were removed from the site returned mysteriously. At another holy well in south-east Cornwall, ST NUN'S WELL (SX 224564) near Pelynt, a large stone bowl with an ornamental rim was twice removed by a farmer, and twice found its own way back. This well is one which is also reputed to have a guardian spirit in the form of an elf-like being, and is often called the Piskey Well.

The stones of Zennor Quoit have the power of returning to their original site
(C. Weatherhill)

These monuments, or their supernatural guardians, also have the ability to exact vengeance upon desecrators. A Georgian farmer once resolved to break up ZENNOR QUOIT to build a cowshed – the corner posts of which still stand close by. He actually succeeded in splitting off the top of one of the pair of giant slabs forming a facade to the dolmen but was persuaded to stop by the local vicar and five shillings. Nevertheless, his fortunes waned, his crops were blighted, his cattle died. At ST NUN'S WELL, the farmer who had removed the stone bowl twice tried for a fateful third time. He lost his wits, was struck dumb, and the oxen he used for dragging the bowl away died.

Blight's engraving of St Nun's Well (The Piskey Well). The ornamented stone bowl can be seen just inside the entrance.

BOSCASWELL HOLY WELL (SW 376347), near Pendeen in West Cornwall, resented being deepened by a local man who was stricken with paralysis for his pains.

One of the most drastic acts of supernatural revenge was that exacted by the holy well at PHILLACK (SW 565384) after being blighted by having a mangy dog washed in it. The deed was carried out in 1720 by Erasmus Pascoe, no less a man than the Sheriff of Cornwall. Pascoe's son died only two months after the event and Erasmus himself suffered a horrible death. His family was reduced to poverty and his branch of that family became extinct within twenty years.

The stones of a curious enclosure called KERRIS ROUNDAGO (SW 445273) were dragged away for the building of a quay at Penzance, but the young healthy draught horses employed for the work died before the destruction of the monument could be completed.

The Merry Maidens Stone Circle (P. Devereux)

In 1861, J. O. Halliwell recorded that an old man told him of a farmer's attempt to remove stones of the MERRY MAIDENS stone circle (SW 433245) near Lamorna Cove. Two of three stones were removed but found their way back into place by morning. Another version says that the oxen which were to drag the stones from their sockets collapsed and died.

The name MERRY MAIDENS was only coined about a century or so ago. Formerly the circle was called "Dauns Myne" ('stone dance'). When

Bottrell compiled his collection of folk-lore and legend c.1870, local folk only knew the tale of girls petrified for dancing on the Sabbath (along with their Pipers and Fiddler, three massive menhirs nearby) from recent books. It was certainly no part of local tradition, and one suspects the Methodists of originating this interpretation. Indeed, the Pipers were always called the Hurlers by locals, because they were used as a goal in this ancient and violent game where "country" played "town" (rural parishioners of St Buryan versus the Churchtown parishioners – the Churchtown cross was the other goal). The name of "Nine Maidens" given to a number of other stone circles is probably also of Methodist origin; at one such circle at BOSKEDNAN (SW 434351) near Madron, the title was unknown in 1700 when it was called "Mein yn dans" ('stones in a dance').

The Hurlers on Bodmin Moor, whose stones, it was said, could not be counted
(C. Weatherhill)

The name of THE HURLERS (SX 258714), three stone circles at Minions on Bodmin Moor, is older, being recorded as such by Norden c.1600. Here it was said that the stones could not be counted: different counts produced different results, even if a penny loaf was placed on each stone in turn.

Some monuments possess the power of healing, most notably the MEN AN TOL (SW 426349) on the Penwith moors north of Madron. The name means "stone of the hole" which aptly describes it. Children suffering from scrofula and rickets would be passed widdershins (anti-clockwise) through the hole, the magical three times: adults with back and limb pains would pass through nine times. It was therefore known alternatively as the Crick Stone (a supposed forked rock of this name mentioned by Hunt and on the boundary of Morvah and Zennor parishes has never existed). It should be added that, despite the assertions of some recent publications, the Men an Tol has never been known as the Devil's Eye. An additional property of the Men an Tol is its ability to act as an oracle. Two brass pins placed crosswise on top of the stone will move apart of their own accord if the answer to a question put to the stone is affirmative.

Another holed stone, the TOLVAN (SW 706283) near Gweek, has similar healing powers but apparently not oracular ones.

The famous TINTAGEL CASTLE (SX 050890) has a peculiar property of its own. Twice a year, the castle – presumably the entire headland – vanishes, perhaps to emerge for a short time in another dimension. Nearby, BOSSINEY MOUND (SX 065888) is a ringwork; the site of an early Norman castle. According to the Rev. Sabine Baring-Gould,

The Tolvan has similar healing powers to the Men-an-tol (P. Devereux)

King Arthur's Round Table puts in a brief appearance each Midsummer Night, when in a blaze of light and a flash of gold, the Table rises from beneath the mound, pauses for a glorious moment and then sinks again.

Some monuments emit sounds. J. C. Tregarthen in "Wild Life at the Land's End" writes of a mound by a reedy pool on a lonely moor near Ding Dong Mine in West Penwith, which was known as "The Deadman". This emits an eerie and desolate shriek in response to a local death. This mound has been identified as the Bronze Age barrow once called TUBAN BROAZE (or TUBMAN BROAZE: SW 437357), which means "great mound". It is easy to see how "tubman" has become corrupted to "deadman" and the silted remains of the pool still exist beside it.

Further to the west, the natural tor of CARN KENIDJACK (SW 388330) is named for the strange sounds which contribute to its weird reputation. The "carn" of the present name appears to be a tautology; the old forms of the name – Carn Usack, Carnidgack etc – show it to mean "hooting tor". In the tale of the wrestling demons (see Chapter 9), it is the chorus of the demonic three-men's song which ends in a piercing hoot: in other accounts the rocks themselves produce the unearthly sound and on occasion, the wind, keening through the gaps in the twisted crags produces a sound of almost human timbre.

The Cornish rocks, particularly the granites, often produce the strangest of formations.

The Logan Rock, on the headland of Treryn Dinas
(C. Weatherhill)

Although natural, a number of these were held to possess strange properties. Loggan stones (now so often misleadingly spelt 'logan'), the rocking stones produced by the weathering of granite which joins both horizontally and vertically, can be of great size and the sight of these huge masses swaying in the wind instilled awe in the ordinary people. Cornwall's largest, the 70 ton LOGAN ROCK (SW 398220) on the headland of Treryn Dinas, was, like the similar stone near Nancegollan, once called Men Amber (mean omber – balanced stone), and sweethearts once climbed up to it to swear vows of fidelity in its name. This and other loggans could not be rocked by those with treachery in their hearts.

The top stone of the Twelve o'clock Stone would rock like a cradle exactly at midnight
(C. Weatherhill)

High on Trink Hill is the TWELVE O'CLOCK STONE (SW 505371), a solid, unmoving mass of granite yet, precisely at midnight, its top stone would rock like a cradle. Children placed on the stone at the magical moment would be cured of rickets and similar diseases, but the stone refused to rock for illegitimate children, or the children of separated or divorced parents. The folk of Nancledra once processed to this stone by a prescribed route which took them through a since-destroyed natural rock arch on the Cuckoo Hill.

One of Cornwall's strangest formations is the famous CHEESEWRING (SX 258724) on Stowe's Hill. The topmost stone of this top-heavy pile was said to revolve three times each time a cock crowed. A stone of "white marble" (quartz?), with rock basins in its surface, once stood on another rock near Looe Harbour (SX 254539). Known as the COCK-CROW STONE, this also turned round three times at the sound of a cock crowing in Hay farmyard close by. This stone has been overthrown and now lies beneath the waters of the Looe.

The Sacrificial Rock on Carn Brea (C. Weatherhill)

Rock basins are, in many places, a feature of granite formations. Once thought to have been artificial, most are now acknowledged as being of natural origin, although it is not beyond the realms of possibility that some might have been enhanced by the hand of man. Two centuries ago, the worthy Dr William Borlase and a number of his contemporaries believed them to have been the work of the Druids and the receptacles of sacrificial blood, although the country folk declared them to be the impress of giants' fingers, or similar.

One of the most remarkable examples is the SACRIFICIAL ROCK (SW 683407) on Carn Brea, a huge oval boulder studded with basins and which also has the name of the "Giant's Crocks and Kettles". Another magnificent example is the piled outcrop called BOSWORLAS LEHAU (SW 378305) near St Just, also called the "Giant's Quoits".

Legends of these basins are few, but to the south of St Just is the squat, toad-like TOM THUMB ROCK (SW 368306), which has a large rock basin. A sinister legend tells that at St Just feast, held close to November 1 – the Celtic festival of Samhain and the Celtic New Year – the first stranger to enter the town was wined and dined, made king for a day, then at sunset, taken out to the Tom Thumb Rock where he was sacrificed. The victim's throat was cut and the blood ran into the basin; thus, the gods were persuaded to ensure the crops in the coming year. A dim memory of this lasted well into this century when a walk to the rock after church was traditional.

14

Leys, Churchways, Spirit Lines and Mythic Routes

No study of a region's mythic themes could be complete without reference to mysterious lines in the landscape. The archaeological "heresy" of leys (or "leylines" as they are now popularly called) is of course the most infamous example of such features, but this term is widely misunderstood, and the true nature of curious lines, linear features and strange trackways in ancient landscapes the world over is only now beginning to be seriously considered. As this chapter attempts to show, different kinds of mystery lines have to be considered in conjunction with one another.

"Leys"

In the 1920s, the respected inventor, businessman, public figure and amateur archaeologist, Alfred Watkins of Hereford gave the name "leys" to alignments formed by ancient sites he considered were deliberately lined up across country. The reasons he chose the Saxon "ley" (cleared land under grass, meadow) for his lines need not concern us here, but we may note that he stopped using it in the 1920s, preferring simply "old straight track" or "archaic track", for Watkins thought his alignments were the remnants of old straight traders' tracks surveyed by line of sight (thus explaining their aligned straightness) in prehistory.

The types of site marking Watkins' lines were varied, and included not only prehistoric monuments such as standing stones and burial mounds but also later features such as pre-Reformation churches. He explained this by claiming that old churches on leys represented the Christianisation of former pagan sites. This certainly did happen, though not to the extent Watkins thought, and we shall see other reasons why "leys" involve churches.

John Michell (centre, with map, leaning on stone) who conducted an important ley survey of West Penwith in the 1970s. Here, he is shown with a standing stone he discovered in 1984 near the Penwith village of Sheffield at SW 45852752 on private farmland. It stands at the junction of three old hedges and Michell found that it fitted in with his 1970s system of lines: it stands in line with the Merry Maidens stone circle and one of the Piper Stones, and it also aligns with stones numbered 7 to 18 in Mitchell's book of his Penwith study: "The Old Stones of Land's End". (P. Devereux)

Watkins, whose main book on the subject of leys was *The Old Straight Track* (1925), died in 1935. The archaeologists of the day dismissed his ideas of prehistoric alignments and straight tracks. This gap between orthodoxy and the "fringe" started to widen immediately after the old Herefordian's death when occult writers began using terms like "lines of force", and dowsers (water diviners or radiesthetists), greatly influenced by the work at that time of French and German dowsers on supposed "geopathological grids", began to claim that leys were lines of a power that could be dowsed. Interest in leys waned over the following decades but came back in force in the psychedelic Sixties, this time decked out with all kinds of colourful associations with UFOs, Atlantis, dowsing and so on, and with the idea of "lines of energy" greatly reinforced. This remains the popular definition, even though it is rooted only in misunderstanding, naivety and unaccountable claims.

Fortunately, behind this public-surface razzmatazz about energy lines, a quieter, landscape-based study of alignments has survived at the core of ley interest. Concurrent with this, modern archaeology has become more conscious of the placing of sites in the landscape as a whole and in investigating mysterious prehistoric "roads", tracks and linear earthworks around the world. So the gap between some branches of "ley hunting" and archaeology is narrowing in certain regards.

An early post-Sixties example of an important landscape-based ley-hunting study was conducted in Cornwall – the Land's End district of West Penwith, to be precise. Writer and researcher John Michell took a new look at the survey of West Penwith conducted by Sir Norman Lockyer early this century. Lockyer was among the first to describe the astronomical attributes of Stonehenge, and had studied celestial orientations of temples in Egypt and Greece: he was the father of "archaeoastronomy", the study of ancient astronomy. In Cornwall he was looking for astronomically significant alignments from stone circles by identifying standing stone outliers to circles that he thought marked key sun, moon and star positions. This work was less rigid than it ought to have been, and came in for criticism, but it was a start. Michell took these surveys and examined the astronomical orientation lines across country. He discovered other standing stones positioned along them, as well as "secondary" points like old Celtic crosses and prehistoric hilltop earthworks.

Michell published his results in *The Old Stones of Land's End* in 1974. Amongst the more interesting findings in this work are the alignments of standing stones apparently radiating out from the greatest of all surviving stone circles in West Penwith, Boscawen-un (SW 413274). One example of these is Lockyer's Line 6 (Michell's Boscawen line III) which marks the November sunrise. The stone Lockyer had identified as the outlier was the pillar at SW 422269, in fields between Trelew Farm and the B3283 road, from where the upper part of the stone is visible. This could never have been seen from Boscawen-un, Michell realised, and found what he claims to be a fallen stone nearer the circle. As well, he went on to find three further stones on the alignment. "Thus," Michell writes, "between the Circle and the sea at Penzer Point are three standing and one, possibly two, fallen stones placed on one straight line." Including the circle, this line is therefore defined by five or six possible contemporaneous markers in about three miles.

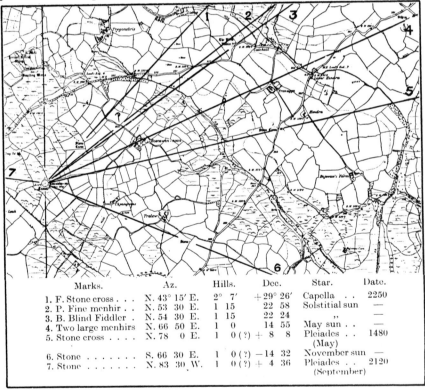

Marks.	Az.	Hills.	Dec.	Star.	Date.
1. F. Stone cross . . .	N. 43° 15′ E.	2° 7′	+29° 26′	Capella . .	2250
2. P. Fine menhir . .	N. 53 30 E.	1 15	22 58	Solstitial sun	—
3. B. Blind Fiddler .	N. 54 30 E.	1 15	22 24	,,	—
4. Two large menhirs	N. 66 50 E.	1 0	14 55	May sun . .	—
5. Stone cross	N. 78 0 E.	1 0 (?) + 8 8		Pleiades . . (May)	1480
6. Stone	S. 66 30 E.	1 0 (?) −14 32		November sun	—
7. Stone	N. 83 30 W.	1 0 (?) + 4 36		Pleiades . . (September)	2120

Sir Norman Lockyer's plan of astronomical alignments from the Boscawen-un stone circle

In 1976, Pat Gadsby and Chris Hutton-Squire subjected Michell's study to computer analysis, in which the map references of the selected West Penwith sites were "nudged" around to create a random pattern. the computer then scanned for any alignments between the randomised "sites". It then scanned all the possible alignments between the actual site positions, accurate to within 10 metres. If the two results were similar, then it would mean that Michell's alignments were no better than chance. In the event, Gadsby and Hutton-Squire found a significantly higher number of alignments among the real sites than among the simulated points (57 against 35). Furthermore, it was found that Michell's lines were much narrower (about one metre), so more accurate, than the 10-metre ones allowed in the computer study. Also, the computer could not take in the additional significance of the astronomical orientations.

That archaeologists can nowadays undertake similar, though admittedly more rigorous, types of study to Michell's West Penwith ley-hunt is shown in *Cornish Archaeology* 29 (1990), where archaeologist Frances Peters reports on her results in testing intervisibility between 95 existing or former menhirs (tall individual standing stones) in West Penwith. She found there was a high degree of intervisibility from any given menhir to others, often over considerable distances, and that groups of menhirs fell into various sighting systems within the peninsula. Peters thinks the stones were used in boundary systems but admits that this would not necessarily "exclude a ritual function".

Churchways and "coffin lines"

Alignments of prehistoric standing stones like those suggested above are "pure" leys, if you like, but it is very clear from a study of Alfred Watkins' own work that many different kinds of lines were included under the general heating of "leys" (which is best used, if at all, in a general or generic sense – there really is no one, single thing that is a "ley"). In particular, Watkins seems to have incorporated churchways or paths in his alignments, and it is this factor more than Christianisation of church sites which probably accounts for the occurrence of old churches on his leys.

In the simplest analysis, churchways were essentially medieval communications between a church and the outlying farmsteads in the parish. They were also "death roads" or "corpse ways" in that the dead would be carried in walking funerals from a farmstead to be buried in the churchyard. There are, however, elements about *some* churchways that suggests they may be remnants of deepter-rooted landscape features that may have been pre-Christian: the line of a churchway may be unusually straight, it may extend through the church and on to prehistoric sites, it may have folklore or mythic associations.

We can see all these elements illustrated in Cornwall, a county especially rich in churchway remnants. Not only do sections of paths survive, but even where they have disappeared a granite stile or a "pathway" fieldname can still tell of the former route of a churchway. Also, nearly all of the abundant old crosses of Cornwall mark the course of churchways (where the crosses still stand in their original positions, that is). They were often the stations where a funeral party would stop and sing specific hymns. It is oral folklore amongst the older inhabitants of West Penwith to call such churchways "coffin lines". (This idea of the "line" in the folk mind is possibly significant, for it hints at a sense of an alignment rather than just a physical feature like a common trackway).

Delightful old Chapel Street in Penzance marks a segment of the line of a churchpath which led from the main church in the town (St Mary's, on the site of an older chapel), on the Pen Sanz or Holy Headland itself, to Madron Church a mile and half to the northwest. Beyond Madron, a half-mile-long straight length of a churchway can be picked up along the same alignment, which exten-

Looking southwards down Chapel Street towards St Mary's church, Penzance (P. Devereux)

ded even further passes through the Neolithic dolmen of Lanyon Quoit. Such a line, marked by segments of road and track, and passing through two old churches and a prehistoric megalith, is indeed remarkably similar to a Watkins ley!

Lanyon Quoit, on the extended alignment of the Penzance – Madron churchway
(P.Devereux)

Bottrell recounts a legend associated with Brea Vean in which a changeling is placed under a stile on a churchway for the fairies to replace with the real baby overnight (see Chapter 2). This hints at unexpected pagan associations with the churchway (or stiles), for the fairies certainly weren't Christian.

Craig Weatherhill, in *The Ley Hunter* 118 (1993), traces in detail a churchway that leads from near St Ives through Zennor, Morvah and Pendeen. He notes that it in fact passes three parish churches, avoiding each one! It is, however, associated with the earlier wayside crosses, suggesting that it emerges out of the Celtic twilight when the pagan traditions were dying but still extant and the Christian ones just beginning to take over but not dominant. Weatherhill further notes that the route seems to have a distinct association with witchcraft, also a possible indication that the route was significant to older religions and beliefs than Christianity. Indeed, Zennor is strongly marked in folklore as a centre of witch activity. In Trewey, next to Zennor, a witch transformed herself into a hare in order to get food from St Ives, five miles away, for her husband's dinner; the route she took was the same as the church-way. (There is even a hamlet called Wicca on the line!)

In *The Ley Hunter* 117 (1992), Gabrielle Hawkes and Tom Henderson-Smith trace a churchway from the church at St Just along segments of track and past wayside crosses through and beyond St Buryan Church (SW 409257). This church has a circular graveyard, and has been proven to mark a prehistoric site.

One of the most atmospheric churchways is the segment that aligns straight to St Levan's church (SW 381222) from the hamlet of Rospletha

(SW 383224), and is marked by two crosses. It is a mythic route, for St Levan was said to be in the habit of following a particular path from the hamlet of Bodellan (SW 382231) to his chapel, below which he used to fish. His route, ''St Levan's Path'', changes direction at Rospletha to align directly to the church. Rospletha is a ''mythologised'' location: one Sunday a woman called Johanna rebuked St levan for going fishing on the Sabbath. The path legend states that ''the grass grows greener wherever the good priest trod than in any other part of the fields through which the footpath

St Levan's Path, viewed from the Rospletha end, looking towards the church. Note the wayside cross (P. Devereux)

passes". When one walks down this saintly path to the church, there is another cross and a *coffin-shaped* stone where it crosses the churchyard boundary -the path is clearly a "coffin line"!

That such paths could have marked ancient routes for untold generations is indicated by the conservatism revealed in the old Cornish saying: "Never carry a corpse to church by a new road".

A full-size coffin-shaped stone at the end of St Levan's Path, where it meets the churchyard boundary (P. Devereux)

St Levan's church is itself old, its building materials said to have been brought to the site by supernatural means (probably along a churchway route, in fact). The pre-Christian significance of the site may have been invested in a curious split boulder to be found in the churchyard. Legend has Christianised it as St Levan's Stone: it is said St Levan split the boulder with a blow from his fist, foretelling that when a pack horse could pass through the cleft with full panniers, it would be the end of the world. The good news is that the crack is still far too narrow for this!

St Levan's Stone

Spirit Lines

All around the world there are similar corpse ways. In Holland there are "Doodwegen" (deathroads) that link hamlets and medieval cemeteries. Some still survive near Hilversum, and are literally "dead straight". Moreover, there were medieval laws which forbade the carriage of corpses to burial in other than straight lines. Way across the world, in Costa Rica, NASA aerial photographic imaging technology has revealed straight Native American paths deep in the rainforest. It turns out that these, too, were for the ritual carriage of the dead. Similar features of Viking vintage have been found in Scandinavia. And so on.

The "dead straight" link seems to go back to ideas of the movement of spirits. In the folklore of certain parts of Germany, for instance, there are accounts of "Geisterwege", perfectly straight but invisible paths linking cemeteries; these paths are haunted by ghosts. Hints of similar beliefs in Cornwall, and the British Isles in general, may be retained in stories of spectral "lane-dogs" like the North Hill example on Bodmin Moor, Devil's lanes like the ancient sunken track near Carn Kenidjack, and ghostly funerals and coaches, like the sinister apparition at Lanreath (recall all these examples from Chapter 9). A similar story involves the ghost of a monk which supposedly haunts a stretch of the A389 road near Little Petherick, close to Padstow. The idea of spirits following particular routes was also certainly indicated by the old practice prevalent throughout northern Europe of placing spirit traps (such as threads laced across hoops) on stakes driven into paths leading to and from cemeteries.

Ley researchers now think that such associations with churchways and other old routes, often straight, go back to very ancient ideas to do with the passage of spirits. The old landscape lines are *spirit lines*, not "energy lines"! Everywhere, the evidence supports this realisation. Just for example, in China there is an archaic system of sacred geography called "Feng shui" in which houses or tombs are not to be built on straight roads or other straight linear features because bad spirits move along them; likewise, in Ireland one doesn't build on the (invisible) straight fairy passes or paths which link prehistoric earthworks or "raths".

Landscape lines are not just imaginary, as Watkins leys are often accused of being by critics. Real, physical mystery lines, many of them clearly deliberately straight, occur worldwide. These include features such as the 1500-year-old, dead straight lines which criss-cross the desert near Nazca, Peru; the 1000-year-old straight "roads" of the lost Anasazi Indians of Chaco Canyon, New Mexico, and in many places throughout the Americas; the 5000-year-old linear earthworks in Britain called "cursuses" that link Neolithic burial mounds, and are now mainly visible only from the air.

(It is thought that the Nazca lines were *ritually swept* during their period of use 1500 years ago. Still practised in the Andes, though now in a Christian context, this sweeping is a way of symbolically creating sacred space, and perhaps parallels the ancient British and northern European folk practice of sweeping disused paths free of haunting spirits with a special flail).

As the unravelling of the mystery of the lines has proceeded, researchers have found similar spirit-and-line ideas associated with threads and string. These, too, are "lines" – we speak of a "fishing line", for example. Australian aborigines used a filament secreted by an insect to act as a "road" for a sick person's spirit to return, and Siberian Buryat shamans did the same thing with red threads.

But what lay behind this deep-rooted "spirit-and-line" concept? Research-based ley hunters feel that because such similar motifs occurred in different cultures and periods, a *cross-cultural* answer has to be sought, and that means one related to the universality of human consciousness, transcending differing societies. Shamanism provides the link, for it was a universal expression of the human mind. It occurred in most parts of the world over vast periods of time, and was a primary experience of human consciousness, not a religion – though it underpinned many of the later great religions. The shaman was the intermediary between the tribe and the spirit worlds. While in the spirit realms, the shaman's soul shared the same nature as the souls of the ancestors, of the dead. The shaman entered the spirit worlds by means of an out-of-body, ecstatic "journey" during trance, induced by a variety of techniques, such as drumming or taking mind-altering plants. The shamanic "flight of the soul" seems to have been translated onto ancient sacred landscapes as straight lines. Some of these were physical, and later became variously acculturated and modified through socio-religious changes to roads of the dead, church lines, triumphal routes and royal roads (monarchy also contains elements of shamanism, and many early kings were supposed to be able to fly). Other lines, such as fairy and ghost paths, were more conceptual than physical.

The *straightness* so often associated with spirit lines is thought to have come, conceptually, from the idea that flight is the straight way over the land – hence "as the crow flies". A similar-meaning phrase is "as straight as an arrow", and both bird and arrow imagery symbolise shamanic spirit flight in tribal art worldwide. Neurologically, the straightness derives from the "entopic" ("within vision") imagery encountered in "out-of-body" trance states. The tunnel entopic pattern, as often reported in Near-Death experiences, is the neurological blue-print that ultimately underlies the "spirit line" at the heart of the whole complex.

This unravelling of the mystery of the lines has only just begun, and is clearly a complex affair with many levels so cannot be told properly here (see Devereux's *Shamanism and the Mystery Lines*, 1992, for a full account). It is important to grasp, however, that no one is suggesting that even the more archaic churchways in Cornwall were for the old Cornish to zip along in out-of-body spirit form! The shaman's soul flight was probably long forgotten as such by the time they were created, having been modified by generations of social and religious change to vague folk superstitions about where ghosts and spirits moved through the landscape and the need for the dead to be conducted to burial along similar special routes. Nevertheless, some notion of spirit flight may have survived into the earlier period of the churchways, for it is known that the use of "flying ointments" made from mind-altering herbs was kept alive in Britain as elsewhere in Europe up until the medieval period by rural wise women. These plant drugs contain alkaloids that specifi-cally produce the hallucinatory sensation of leaving one's body, and the image of the witch flying on her broomstick (or Madge Figgy flying on a stem of ragwort) is thought to derive from this. The flying witch was at the tail end of an earlier tradition, that of the "myrkrida", or rider in the dark, which in turn was probably a last vestige of some archaic form of European shamanism. In the myrkrida tradition there were only certain places where the night-flying wise-women could cross fences or hedges (juniper was often put into hedges by superstitious rural folk because it was thought to protect against witchcraft): one could speculate wildly that some churchway stiles mark such points ...

Mythic Routes

St Levan's Path is a small-scale example of a *mythic route*. Cornish folklore yields many more examples, large and small, for legend does not only define specific events and locations, it can identify specific links between places. Such mythic routes are remarkably akin to the "dream journey routes" or "songlines" of the Australian Aborigine. These are tribally-known but invisible ways through the Outback that the Aborigines follow at certain times, tracing the journeys of the Dreamtime creation heroes. These Dreamtime beings are remarkably similar to the giants, and the saints-as-giants, that figure in Cornish folklore.

Following, in abbreviated form, are just some of the Cornish mythic routes and geographical connections recorded in the folklore. Many of them the reader will recall encountering earlier in this book.

The giant Bolster could stand with one foot on St Agnes Beacon (SW 709506) and the other on Carn Brea (SW 685406). These two hills are six miles apart. Another legend says that Bolster and the giant who lived on Carn Brea threw rocks at one another. A third mythological link between the two places is supplied by the Giant's Head or Face Rock (SW 687409) on Carn Brea which when viewed from the west resembles a face staring out towards the coast and St Agnes Beacon.

Nancy Trenoweth was carried on a horse ridden by the ghost of her lover, Frank Lanyon, from Kemyel (SW 461251) via Trewoofe (SW 439254) to St Buryan churchyard (SW 409257).

The giants of Trencrom Hill (SW 518362) and St Michael's Mount used to play "bob-buttons": the Mount was the "bob" on which granite slabs were placed to serve as "buttons", and Trencrom was the "mit" or the spot from which the throw was made. Another legend says that the giants of Trencrom and the Mount had only one cobbling hammer between them, so to share it they threw it to one another.

The Devil, or alternatively the Bucca, flew from Paul Hill (SW 465271) to Tolcarne (SW 461293) above Newlyn, where he turned the fishermen's nets into stone.

During a stay at St Keverne's hermitage on the Lizard peninsula, St Just stole a rare cup from his host. He ran off back towards his hermitage in St Just, via Breage (SW 619284), with St Keverne in hot pursuit throwing ironstone boulders at him. These dropped by the roadside between Breage and Germoe, where St Just also flung down his ill-gotten gain in order to better make his escape.

When at home (SW 372315), the delinquent St Just used to throw rocks at St Sennen at SW 357255 who threw rocks back in retaliation. One one occasion the rocks collided in mid air, fused together and fell near Bosavern (SW 370304).

The ghost of a drowned woman appearing as a ball of light used to travel nightly from Chair Ladder (SW 365217) to the hamlet of Raftra (SW 376233).

A giant who lived at the hill fort of Warbstow Bury (SX 202908) was killed by a tool thrown at him by the giant of Launceston Castle.

The legend of Pee Tregeer, who was able to see a fairy at Penzance market due to her illicit use of a greenish ointment, is very specific about the route she took back home from Penzance to Pendeen – "she didn't return by Polteggan Bottom and Boswednan, though it's the nearest". Instead, she went via Castle Horneck fields (SW 457303), "three or four miles" on the high road, Boslow (SW 396327), the Gump near Carn Kenidjack (where she was piskey-led and encountered amongst other things little folk with a goblet in the shape of a poppy capsule – (an opium reference?) and finally Pendeen (SW 387346).

Most of these mythic routes or connections are presented in the form of flying or throwing actions, thus a straight or direct route is implied. Even where three or more locations are specified on a land journey, there is often a "broad-band" directness.

These kind of legends draw the "songlines" across the mythic landscape of the Cornish Dreamtime.

Select Bibliography

Books

ASHE, Geoffrey	*The Mythology of the British Isles*, 1990
BARING-GOULD, Rev. S.:	*Cornish Characters and Strange Events*, 1925
BLIGHT, J.T.	*A Week at the Land's End*, 1861
BORD, Janet and Colin	*Earth Rites*, 1982
	Sacred Waters, 1985
BOTTRELL, William	*Traditions & Hearthside Stories* (3 vols.), 1870-1880
BRIGGS, Katherine	*A Dictionary of Fairies*, 1976
COLQUHOUN, Ithel	*The Living Stones*, 1957
COOKE, Ian	*Journey to the Stones*, 1987
COURTNEY, Margaret	*Cornish Feasts and Folklore*, 1890
DEVEREUX, Paul	*Earth Lights Revelation*, 1989
	Places of Power, 1990
	Shamanism & the Mystery Lines, 1992
	Symbolic Landscapes, 1993
DITMAS, E.M.R.	*Tristan and Iseult in Cornwall*, 1969
DEURR, Hans Peter	*Dreamtime*, 1978 (Eng. Lang. edition 1985/91)
GENDALL, R.R.M.	*An Curnoack Hethow* (2nd edition), 1993
GRINSELL, Leslie V.	*Folklore of Prehistoric Sites in Britain*, 1976
HALLIWELL, J.O.	*Rambles in Western Cornwall*, 1861

HAMILTON JENKIN, A.J.	*Cornwall & Its People* (3 vols), 1932-1934
HARNER, Michael (Ed.)	*Hallucinogens and Shamanism,* 1973
HARRIS, J. Henry	*Cornish Saints and Sinners,* 1906
HIRTH, Eric	*Ghosts in Cornwall,* 1986
HUNT, Robert	*Romances and Superstitions of the West of England,* 1881
JAMES, Beryl	*Tales of the Tinners' Way,* 1988
	Tales of the Saints' Way, 1993
JOHN, C.R.	*The Saints of Cornwall,* 1981
JOHNS, Rev. C.A.	*A Week at the Lizard,* 1848
LANE-DAVIES, A.	*Holy Wells of Cornwall,* 1976
"LYONESSE"	*Legend Land* (4 vols), 1922
McEWAN, Graham J.	*Haunted Churches of England,* 1989
MEYRICK, J.	*A Pilgrim's Guide to the Holy Wells of Cornwall,* 1982
MICHELL, John	*The Old Stones of Land's End,* 1974
MORTON NANCE, R.	*A Glossary of Cornish Sea-Words,* 1963
PADEL, O.J.	*The Cornish Background of the Tristan Stories,* 1981
PENNICK, Nigel, and DEVEREUX, Paul	*Lines on the Landscape,* 1989
QUILLER-COUCH, M.L.	*Ancient and Holy Wells of Cornwall,* 1894
ROSS, Anne	*Druids, Gods & Heroes from Celtic Mythology,* 1986
SPOONER, Barbara	*Jan Tregeagle, Man & Ghost* (undated, reprinted 1977)
STANIER, Peter	*The Work of Giants,* 1988
TREGARTHEN, Enys	*Legends and Tales of North Cornwall,* 1890
WATKINS, Alfred	*The Old Straight Track,* 1925 (1970)

WEATHERHILL, Craig   *Belerion: Ancient Sites of Land's End*, 1981

                          Cornovia: Ancient Sites of Cornwall & Scilly,
                          1985

                          The Lyonesse Stone, 1991

                          Seat of Storms, 1994

WHITFELD, Rev. H.J.   *Scilly and its Legends*, 1852

Magazines and Journals

Journal of the Royal Institution of Cornwall (annual)

Meyn Mamvro: Ancient Stones and Sacred Sites in Cornwall (quarterly)

Old Cornwall: Journal of the Federation of Old Cornwall Societies (quarterly)

The Ley Hunter (quarterly)

Index

Explore the countryside with Sigma!

We have a wide selection of guides to individual towns, plus outdoor activities centred on walking and cycling in the great outdoors throughout England and Wales. Perfect companions to this book are:

PUB WALKS IN CORNWALL - Laurence Main

PUB WALKS ON EXMOOR - Philip Pond

PUB WALKS ON DARTMOOR - Laurence Main

PUB WALKS IN SOUTH DEVON - Laurence Main

Plus dozens more 'Pub Walks' books for just about every popular walking area in the UK, all featuring access by public transport. All priced at £6.95

Students of the mystical and supernatural will also enjoy:

SHADOWS: a northern investigation of the unknown - Steve Cliffe (£7.95)

MYSTERIES OF THE MERSEY VALLEY - Peter Hough and Jenny Randles (£7.95)

GHOSTS, TRADITIONS AND LEGENDS OF OLD LANCASHIRE - Kenneth Howarth (£7.95)

MYTHS AND LEGENDS OF WALES - Laurence Main (Autumn 1994 - £7.95)

MAGIC, MYTHS AND MEMORIES: in and around the Peak District - Doug Pickford (£7.95)

MYTHS AND LEGENDS OF EAST CHESHIRE AND THE MOORLANDS - Doug Pickford (£5.95)

. . . with more to come during 1994!

There are many books for outdoor people in our catalogue, including:

RAMBLES IN NORTH WALES
– Roger Redfern

HERITAGE WALKS IN THE PEAK DISTRICT
– Clive Price

EAST CHESHIRE WALKS
– Graham Beech

WEST CHESHIRE WALKS
– Jen Darling

WEST PENNINE WALKS

– Mike Cresswell

NEWARK AND SHERWOOD RAMBLES
– Malcolm McKenzie

RAMBLES AROUND NOTTINGHAM & DERBY
– Keith Taylor

RAMBLES AROUND MANCHESTER
– Mike Cresswell

WESTERN LAKELAND RAMBLES
– Gordon Brown

WELSH WALKS:
Dolgellau and the Cambrian Coast
– Laurence Main and Morag Perrott

WELSH WALKS:
Aberystwyth and District
– Laurence Main and Morag Perrott

– all of these books are currently £6.95 each

Our series of cycling books includes:

CYCLE UK! The definitive guide to leisure cycling - Les Lumsdon (£9.95)

OFF-BEAT CYCLING & MOUNTAIN BIKING IN THE PEAK DISTRICT
– Clive Smith (£6.95)

MORE OFF-BEAT CYCLING IN THE PEAK DISTRICT
– Clive Smith (£6.95)

50 BEST CYCLE RIDES IN CHESHIRE
– edited by Graham Beech (£7.95)

CYCLING IN THE COTSWOLDS
– Stepehn Hill (£6.95)

BY-WAY TRAVELS SOUTH OF LONDON
– Geoff Marshall (£7.95)

BY-WAYS BIKING IN THE CHILTERNS (£7.95)
– Henry Tindell

– plus many more entertaining and educational books being regularly added to our list. All of our books are available from your local bookshop. In case of difficulty, or to obtain our complete catalogue, please contact:

Sigma Leisure, 1 South Oak Lane, Wilmslow, Cheshire SK9 6AR

Phone: 0625 – 531035   Fax: 0625 – 536800

ACCESS and VISA orders welcome – call our friendly sales staff or use our 24 hour Answerphone service! Most orders are despatched on the day we receive your order – you could be enjoying our books in just a couple of days.